UNBREAKABLE

UNBREAKABLE

SAINTS WHO INSPIRED SAINTS
TO MORAL COURAGE

Kimberly Begg

Foreword by
Leila Miller

TAN Books
Gastonia, North Carolina

Cover design by Caroline Green

Cover image: Joan of Arc, 1865 (oil on canvas), Millais, John Everett (1829-96) / English, Photo © Peter Nahum at The Leicester Galleries, London / Bridgeman Images

Library of Congress Control Number: 2023931630

ISBN: 978-1-5051-2609-9
Kindle ISBN: 978-1-5051-2610-5
ePUB ISBN: 978-1-5051-2611-2

Published in the United States by
TAN Books
PO Box 269
Gastonia, NC 28053
www.TANBooks.com

Printed in the United States of America

Lovingly dedicated to my husband, Ian, and our children.

Contents

Foreword

If I have said one thing to Catholic parents over the past few years, it's this: we need confidence and courage to face the spiritual dangers of an increasingly hostile culture—not just for our own souls but for the souls of our children.

We cannot give what we don't have, and courage is in short supply today. The world hates Christ and His Church more than ever, and many Catholics are weary of the battle, often unwilling to undergo the real and painful consequences of taking a public stand for the Faith. This weariness has led some parents to close their eyes to the accelerating moral chaos that threatens to sweep away our children.

To be sure, a good portion of this "slumber" by Catholic parents is more like paralysis, the result of an unspoken fear. Parents are secretly afraid of what will become of their children in an increasingly merciless and perverse society; they don't know if their children can withstand the pressures and temptations that surround them; some even wonder if there is a way around the cross—a way for their children to please both Christ and the world.

"After all," they rationalize, "doesn't God want my children to be happy? To make a good living? To thrive in the world?"

Confusion, complacency, and fear cause even faithful parents to sleep through the war that wages around us and targets our children's souls.

It is high time to awake for battle, and Kimberly Begg has met us with a herald of trumpets! In *Unbreakable*, Begg equips and challenges parents to fulfill their duties to God by setting their children's hearts on fire for Christ. The stories in this book are important and compelling. They will leave parents and children awestruck and eager to serve as soldiers for Christ in our own troubled and dangerous times.

In addition, this book reinforces a critical lesson for modern parents: to whatever crosses we are called, we are not asked to do anything the saints before us have not also done, knowing Christ has gone before us all.

Through the simple genius of *Unbreakable*, Begg has provided something refreshing and invaluable to anxious Catholic parents everywhere: not only the clarity of *truth and faith* but also the inspiration to have *courage and confidence* to back it up.

Leila Miller
Feast of Saint Padre Pio

Preface

When my children were very young, I read a secular parenting book that shared a compelling insight: families that pass on the stories of their ancestors have children who are more confident and well-grounded than those that lack a culture rooted in the past. I immediately saw the parallel to Catholicism. I thought, "What a gift our faith is to all of the world's children!" Indeed, how fortunate we are to be connected to the great saints—the luminaries of the Church who came before us—to model the truth that "Jesus Christ is the same yesterday and today and for ever" (Heb 13:8).

What occupies our children's imaginations is of profound importance. The ideas they ponder and the stories they turn over in their heads—about heroes, honor, sacrifice, and glory—shape the way they see the world and their place in it.

My children attend faithfully Catholic schools where all aspects of the culture and curriculum are rooted in truth. They encounter the Blessed Sacrament daily at Mass and in prayer. They learn about God's world and the human experience through the study of theology, philosophy, science, classic literature, history, mathematics, the arts, and other disciplines.

They also celebrate the lives of the saints. I have seen my children become captivated by the stories of saints they discovered at school—holy men and women who united their wills to the will of God, heroically standing up for the truth of the Catholic faith. What a blessing it is to be a part of school communities that reinforce what we're teaching at home.

I wrote this book to be a resource for Catholic parents, regardless of whether their children attend faithfully Catholic schools, to help them provide a Catholic education for their children. The *Catechism of the Catholic Church* provides important insights about the educational and evangelical duties of parents:

> Parents must regard their children as *children of God.*
> . . . Showing themselves obedient to the will of the Father in Heaven, parents must educate their children to discover their vocation and fulfill God's law. . . .
> . . . Parents have a grave responsibility to give good example to their children. . . .
> . . . Parents must teach children to avoid the compromising and degrading influences that threaten human societies. . . .
> *Education in the faith* should begin in the child's earliest years. . . .
> Parents' respect and affection are expressed by the care and attention they devote to bringing up their young children and *providing for their physical and spiritual needs.* As the children grow up, the same respect and devotion lead parents to educate them in the right use of reason and freedom.[1]

The vocation of Christian parenthood imposes lifelong obligations rooted in the reality that children don't belong to their parents; they belong to God. Fathers and mothers have a duty to raise children who know who they are and why they were made—who know that God is constantly calling them to cooperate with His unique plan for their lives, and who accept and even embrace the suffering and sacrifice required of them on their path to heaven.

It is of paramount importance that parents teach their children to discern and do God's will. Their souls—and their children's souls (and their children's children's souls, and so on)—depend on it.

TAN Books is the perfect home for this book. Since 1967, TAN's number one priority has been the salvation of souls. As such, TAN occupies a unique space in the publishing world, preserving and promoting more than one thousand works aimed at helping God's children to become saints.

In 2021, TAN released *Parenting for Eternity: A Guide to Raising Children in Holy Mother Church* by Conor Gallagher, CEO of TAN. *Parenting for Eternity* is an important work that challenges parents to understand "the eternal consequence of every single parental act—acts of commission and acts of omission"—in forming their children's eternal souls.

Unbreakable: Saints Who Inspired Saints to Moral Courage reinforces Gallagher's crucial message. In keeping with TAN's rich tradition of preserving the Church's teachings and history with the aim of saving souls, this book tells the stories of Church heroes like they've never been told before: with an emphasis on the importance of passing down stories of the saints to help parents cultivate moral courage in their children.

Saints inspire saints. This book attempts to make that point by highlighting a crucial lesson: the men and women who attain heaven are those who love Christ so fiercely that they develop a habit of suffering and sacrificing for Him, fearlessly uniting their wills with His will. I wrote this book to help parents fulfill their duties to their children in a world that is increasingly hostile to Christians. My hope is that it will inspire parents and children alike on their path to heaven.

Acknowledgments

It's incredibly satisfying to look back on how this book came about and know that I owe its fruition to the help of so many wonderful people. Of those, I am most grateful to my loving husband, Ian, who has been amazingly supportive of what may have seemed like an impossible idea at the outset. Despite our many responsibilities at home, he patiently gave me time and space to write without distraction for hours at a time as he did all the things with our mostly happy children. He was the first person to read each chapter, and he offered feedback that made my editor's job much easier.

Which brings me to the second person I need to thank: my editor, Paul Kengor. This book would not have happened without Paul. He is the first person I shared the idea for the book with. He understood the vision and took it to Patrick O'Hearn at TAN Books, who encouraged me to submit a formal proposal. I will forever be grateful to Paul, Patrick, and the hardworking team at TAN, who took a leap of faith in supporting me as a first-time author and bringing me into the TAN family. I am still amazed and so very grateful.

Several friends made important contributions that should be recognized. I would like to express my heartfelt gratitude to Ron Robinson for introducing me to Blessed Jerzy Popiełuszko, whose heroism served as the initial inspiration for the book; Austin Ruse, for reviewing my proposal to TAN; Kevin Doak, for loaning me his extensive Saint Maximilian Kolbe library and for reviewing the section on Kolbe; Catherine Pakaluk, for keeping me accountable for daily word counts, which allowed me to finish writing on Saint Teresa of Calcutta's feast day; and Leila Miller, for reviewing my manuscript and writing such a thoughtful and powerful foreword.

In addition, I would like to thank my parents, Mike and Dee Martin, for baptizing me in the Catholic Church; my children—Charlie, Bryson, Adelyn, Marielle, and Lucia—for giving me a glimpse of the magnificent love that God has for His children; the wonderful priests in my life—especially Fr. Thomas Petri, OP, STD, Fr. Dominic Legge, OP, Fr. Jerry J. Pokorsky, Fr. Mark E. Moretti, Fr. J. D. Jaffe, Fr. Stephen Holmes, and Fr. Matt Russick, TOR—for deepening my relationship with Christ through the sacraments and their examples of holiness; my children's schools—The Heights School in Potomac, Maryland and Holy Family Academy in Manassas, Virginia—for supporting Ian and me in our role as primary educators; and many friends, too many to name, who supported me during this process, and especially those who prayed for me. Special thanks to Mike and Liz Ortner, Rich and Shirley Walker, Hope Hargadon, Ann Woodson, Heather Hambleton, Meg White, Becca Hanssen, Holly Smith, and Beth Sullivan.

Finally, I am most grateful to God for the beautiful gift of my life and the hope of my salvation, and to the Blessed Mother and all the angels and saints for their heavenly assistance. It took me a full year to write the manuscript for this book. I prayed throughout that time and was intentional about praying to the saints as I was writing about them. This may be bold to assert, but I believe the saints featured in this book helped me tell their stories the way they wanted them to be told.

Introduction

Catholic parents have long sought to raise saints. We bring our children to Mass, prioritize the sacraments, and teach them to be Christ-like in their interactions with others. Many of us send our children to Catholic schools and cultivate friendships with Catholic families. We give our children a foundation of faith, which we hope and pray is strong enough to resist the unholy temptations outside our homes.

The world that awaits our children is remarkably different than the one today's parents encountered when they left their childhood homes. It's a world that not only glorifies sin but also demands universal and unequivocal celebration of sin. While the ridiculing of Christians has gone on for decades, the "canceling" of believers as "haters," disqualified from friendships, jobs, and other opportunities, is new.

To prepare our children, we must seek to raise not only saints but *martyrs*—young men and women strong enough to rejoice in the blessings promised by Jesus in Matthew 5:10–12: "Blessed are those who are persecuted for righteousness' sake, for theirs is the kingdom of heaven. Blessed

1

are you when men revile you and persecute you and utter all kinds of evil against you falsely on my account. Rejoice and be glad, for your reward is great in heaven, for so men persecuted the prophets who were before you."

Parents need to be intentional about cultivating moral courage in their children to prepare the next generation of Christians to stand up for their faith amidst the hostility of an increasingly atheistic and antagonistic culture.

G. K. Chesterton—the renowned twentieth-century writer, philosopher, and historian whose love of truth fueled his conversion to Catholicism—said, "The Catholic Church is the only thing that frees a man from the degrading slavery of being a child of his age."[2] Chesterton was masterful at illuminating the brilliant truths of the Catholic faith—but how confusing his words must be to modern people who are ignorant of the history of man and the Church!

The truth of our faith is much more interesting than the modern lens through which most of us have been taught to see the world. The Magisterium of the Catholic Church recognizes Christ as the Logos—the divine reason for creation, giving the world order, form, and meaning. With Christ as Logos, Christians understand our time in this world as temporary and, at the same time, important and consequential.

All Catholic parents hope and pray their children will live holy lives and go to heaven. Where many parents fall short is preparing their children for what will be required of them as Christians today—sacrificing, suffering, and facing persecution for the faith.

It's no wonder. Catholic parents—even the most devout—are a product of the modern world. And the modern world values happiness above all else, especially concerning children. A recent survey found that 73 percent of Americans rated happiness as the most important goal in raising children and assessing the results of education—far ahead of any other option.[3]

It is not wrong to seek happiness. On the contrary, as Saint John Paul II observed, we are ordered, in Christ, to want and to attain happiness: "People are made for happiness. Rightly, then, you thirst for happiness. Christ has the answer to this desire of yours. But He asks you to trust Him."[4] The problem is that modern parents seek happiness for their children on the world's terms, not God's terms, despite Jesus's instruction in John 15:18–19: "If the world hates you, know that it has hated me before it hated you. If you were of the world, the world would love its own; but because you are not of the world, but I chose you out of the world, therefore the world hates you."

"Hate" is a word that has become all-too familiar to our modern ears. In a world obsessed with wokeness and the celebration of sexual deviancy, "hate" is the secular culture's go-to accusation aimed at silencing and marginalizing Christians. One marvels at the success of a tactic so obviously rooted in deceit, manipulation, and intimidation. After all, "God is love" (1 Jn 4:8). And yet, we know in our hearts that the father of lies has been assisted in his persecution of Christians not only by enemies of Christ and His Church but also by Christians afraid to sacrifice and suffer.

Fear is a terrible reason to risk the salvation of our souls. It's an even worse reason to risk the salvation of our children's souls.

There's no question that raising children today is more complicated than it has been in recent decades, if perhaps ever. Modern parents face challenges to their authority—and God's authority—that their own parents could have never imagined. Indeed, children today are fed a constant narrative celebrating the "courage" and "pride" of people who identify as "LGBTQ+" and condemning the "bigotry" and "hatred" of Christians who uphold biblical truths. It is critical that parents minimize children's exposure to corrupting influences to the greatest extent possible; government schools and modern media should be avoided entirely if possible. But shielding children from the world when they are young is not enough. In order to set them on the path to heaven, parents must also prepare children to stand up for truth once they encounter the world.

Jesus understood that the weaknesses of man include our pitiable desire to be liked—even by a world that despises the source of all love. He knew Christians throughout the ages would try to justify "getting along" with the world in denial of truth in order to avoid sacrifice and suffering. That's why, when He prepared the apostles to go out into the world to proclaim the Kingdom of God, Jesus left them with this warning: "So every one who acknowledges me before men, I also will acknowledge before my Father who is in heaven; but whoever denies me before men, I also will deny before my Father who is in heaven" (Mt 10:32–33).

Our children will be tested in little ways—including conversations with friends and acquaintances—and in big ways that could cost them opportunities to advance in their careers or participate in community life.

Catholic parents must cultivate moral courage in their children. The best way to do this is to pass on stories of the saints who exhibited exceptional courage in their times—including red martyrs, who died for the Faith, and white martyrs, who were persecuted by a world hostile to the Faith—in a manner that engages children's minds and excites their imaginations.

Similar to Sacred Scripture and Church teaching, the stories of the saints are the birthright of all Catholic children. They make up an essential part of the Church's education tradition. They have been passed down by dutiful parents since the earliest days of the Church, inspiring successive generations of saints willing to endure persecution for Christ.

This book tells the stories of some of the Church's most courageous saints—and the saints who inspired them:

Saint Joan of Arc was the fifteenth-century French teenager who fulfilled God's extraordinary plan for her life, leading French troops to drive the English out of Orléans, making it possible for Charles VII, the rightful heir to the French throne, to be coronated in Reims and ultimately save France from English rule. She was betrayed by her countrymen and her king, captured by the English, and forced to endure underhanded interrogations and a sham trial resulting in her burning at the stake. Under the threat of torture and an agonizing death, she refused to affirm the lies of her indictment and conviction.

Before Joan could save France, she needed the courage to leave her home and subject herself to the ridicule of asking the captain of a royal fortress to help her—a sixteen-year-old farm girl—obtain an army to command. The journey marked the beginning of a three-year period when Joan practiced acts of courage on and off the battlefield every day.

When Joan was fourteen years old, Saint Michael the Archangel, Saint Margaret of Antioch, and Saint Catherine of Alexandria visited her, relaying the extraordinary role God intended her to play in the war, and providing encouragement and counsel. Saint Michael is the commander of God's army and protector of the Church who defeated the unholy angels in the first great battle between good and evil. Saints Margaret and Catherine were fourth-century teenage martyrs who refused to renounce their faith during the Diocletian persecution, the last and most horrific Roman persecution of Christians. Their love for Christ over their own lives converted thousands of pagans to Christianity.

Saint José Luis Sánchez del Río was the twentieth-century, fourteen-year-old Mexican martyr who served the Cristero army as a Soldier of Christ and was tortured and murdered by the socialist, anti-Catholic government. He is one of twenty-five Mexican martyrs who died at the hands of government enforcers as a result of President Plutarco Elias Calles's outlawing of Catholicism (resulting in the execution and exile of priests, seizing of Church property, closure of Catholic schools, and other human rights violations).

Throughout his short life, José showed extraordinary courage in defending Christ against His enemies. When he was a boy, he risked his life by providing "illegal" religious instruction to the children in his town, even taking them to visit Jesus, really present, in the Blessed Sacrament. Desperate to join the Cristero cause, he journeyed a great distance to two camps; he was turned away from the first for being too young and accepted into the second to serve as an aid to General Ruben Guizar Morfin. When General Morfin's horse was shot during a battle, he gave his horse to the general, knowing it would lead to his capture. For six days, the enemy used temptation and the threat of death to try to convince José to renounce his faith. He never wavered.

José grew up with a strong devotion to Our Lady of Guadalupe, who appeared to Saint Juan Diego—a native Mexican, Aztec-to-Catholic convert—in the sixteenth century. Juan Diego showed tremendous courage and persistence in obeying the Blessed Mother. José heard the stories of Anacleto González Flores and Saint Tarcisius at critical times during his life; he made the decision to enlist with the Cristeros soon after visiting Flores's grave. At camp, the soldiers affectionately gave him the nickname "Tarcisius" after the twelve-year-old early Christian who was martyred for protecting the Eucharist.

Blessed Jerzy Popiełuszko was the twentieth-century Polish priest in communist Poland who served as chaplain of the Solidarity Movement. He preached the truth of the Faith, telling the Polish people that the communist state was illegitimate because it violated the dignity owed to all people as children of God, when he knew it made him a target and when it was clear his life was in danger. He was murdered by three security police officers in 1984.

Jerzy never let the communists come between him and his duties to Christ. As a child, he attended daily Mass and served as an altar boy, despite warnings from his communist school that he would receive a lower mark because of his religious activities. During his two years of compulsory military service, he prayed the Rosary out loud even though prayer of any kind was prohibited. He also defied an order to trample on a medal of the Blessed Mother (whom he provocatively identified to the guards as the Queen of Poland). His acts of resistance earned him repeated beatings and other punishments, including a month-long period of solitary confinement. These experiences early in his life helped him develop a habit of courage, even as communists stepped up their harassment and intimidation (apprehending and arresting him thirteen times, planting evidence in his apartment, slandering him in the press, and throwing a bomb into his apartment window).

Jerzy grew up learning about the saints. His favorite saint was Maximilian Kolbe, the Polish Franciscan friar who volunteered to take the place of a Catholic family man when he was sentenced to die in a starvation cell at Auschwitz during World War II. As a teenager attending secondary school, his favorite works were books by Maximilian Kolbe and Cardinal Wyszyński, who was a strong figure of resistance to the Sovietization of Poland. He was trained and ordained by Cardinal Wyszyński at a seminary in Warsaw.

Six years after his ordination, he was part of a massive audience that had come to see Pope John Paul II on his historic visit to Poland in 1978; he sat in one of the front rows.

Saint Teresa of Calcutta was the twentieth-century Albanian-born founder of the Missionaries of Charity who used her popularity as a humanitarian serving the "poorest of the poor" to courageously speak out against the evil of abortion. Born Agnes Gonxha Bojaxhiu, she was known simply as "Mother Teresa" to the world.

Mother Teresa practiced courage every day of her ministry, beginning when she left home at age eighteen to travel to Paris and then India to join the Loreto Order of Irish nuns. When she was thirty-seven years old, she left the safety and security of her religious community to begin a one-person ministry in the streets of Calcutta. What began as a makeshift slum school and hut for the sick and dying in one city grew into a worldwide humanitarian effort operating on six continents just two decades later. Thanks to the interest of a British journalist, she began receiving recognition and awards for her good work. In 1979, she used her platform as the recipient of the Nobel Peace Prize to condemn abortion as "the greatest destroyer of peace today" and the nations that had legalized abortion as "the poorest nations"; Norway, the host country of the distinguished prize, was one of those nations. Throughout the last eighteen years of her life, she took every opportunity to speak out in defense of unborn children, even when it was controversial, including in front of her pro-abortion hosts, President Bill Clinton and First Lady Hillary Clinton, at the National Prayer Breakfast in Washington, DC, in 1994.

When Agnes became a postulant with the Loreto Order, she chose the name "Sister Mary Teresa of the Child Jesus" in honor of Saint Thérèse of Lisieux, the beloved nineteenth-century Carmelite nun, known affectionately as the Little Flower, who professed a spirituality of doing the ordinary with extraordinary love for God. Her autobiography, *Story of a Soul*, contains beautiful and inspiring insights about loving Christ and being "not afraid of suffering for Thee."

***

Before He ascended into heaven, Jesus told His disciples, "I am with you always" (Mt 28:20). For two thousand years—through the persecution of Christians by gruesome killings, ostracization, and ridicule—He has kept His promise, providing a gateway from our fallen world to the kingdom of heaven. All the while, He has raised up saints. In the darkest moments of world history, Christ's light has shined brightly through courageous men and women who refused to be slaves to the lies of their times; they boldly united their wills to the will of God and found their eternal reward in heaven. The stories contained in these pages are a part of the birthright of all Catholics. May they stir the imaginations of today's young people—and inspire them to live a heroic life with Jesus, "always."

Saint Joan of Arc

Joan of Arc is one of history's most fascinating figures. Since the fifteenth century, she has captivated the imagination of people worldwide as each new generation has added to the enormous collection of books, poems, paintings, documentaries, and other works telling her story. Historical records provide an abundance of primary source material. Through transcripts of her two trials and accompanying documents, more evidentiary details are known about her life than that of any person who lived up to her time.[5]

Joan was an illiterate teenaged farm girl who had no connections to the military or French nobility. And yet, when she was sixteen years old, she left home for the singular purpose of commanding a French army, defeating the English in battle, and leading King Charles VII to Reims for his coronation, thus liberating France from English rule. That she accomplished such an outrageous mission is as remarkable as the fact that she embarked on it at all.

It may not have appeared so at first, but Joan had all she needed to save her beloved nation. She had heavenly assistance. For three years before embarking on her mission, she received guidance and inspiration from Saint Michael the Archangel, Saint Catherine of Alexandria, and Saint Margaret of Antioch—three saints who helped her draw closer to God through prayer and the sacraments. Through their intercession, she came to know, accept, and embrace the divine plan for her life: she would be the instrument through which God would save France, and she would do it with His help and on His terms. In obedience, Joan persevered through physical and emotional anguish. She was betrayed by her countrymen, abandoned by her king, and convicted of heresy by the Catholic Church, suffering through a farcical trial that resulted in a death sentence. Innocent of all charges and never wavering in her faith, Joan was burned alive at the stake.

Once, at the beginning of her journey, Joan was asked how she would make it to the king when the road she needed to take was fraught with danger from the enemy. Her answer reflects a deep faith that could transform the perspective of embattled Christians today: "I'm not afraid," she said. "God is with me. I was born to do this."[6]

Childhood

Joan of Arc—named Jehanne by her parents and affectionately called Jeanette—was born on or about January 6, 1412. People in medieval times did not keep birth records as we do today, but they did observe the feasts of the Church.[7] It is thus fitting that Joan's birthday is commemorated on January 6, the feast of the Epiphany. This is the day the Church celebrates the revelation that the infant Jesus was the Savior of the world and the King of heaven and earth. When Joan was an infant, no one in her life knew she was destined to be the savior of France and imitate Jesus's life-giving love, suffering a passion of her own in obedience to God's will. Her parents, however, knew her heavenly destiny, and so they raised their daughter to recognize her Savior's presence in her life.

Jacques d'Arc and Isabelle Romée lived on fifty acres of farmland and pasture in Domrémy, a village in northeastern France. They were faithful Catholics and hard workers,[8] raising three sons and two daughters[9] to love God and live a life of service for Christ. Joan was fourth born of the five children. She was a good, pious, sweet-natured girl. What she learned about faith, virtue, and the ways of the world, she heard at home and church, since she did not receive a formal education and did not know how to read. Her mother taught her the Pater Noster, Ave Maria, and the Credo.[10]

Much of Joan's childhood was spent doing chores. She dutifully helped her mother, following her instruction to help with the spinning, sewing, and housework. She also helped her father on the farm, ploughing the fields, caring for crops, and feeding and guarding cattle.[11]

When she was not helping her parents, Joan often visited churches and other sacred sites. She frequently went to Mass and confession. Nearly every Saturday, she went on pilgrimage to the hermitage of Notre Dame de Bermont to light candles. She gave alms to the poor and cared for the sick. The townspeople admired Joan's goodness and piety. The parish priest said he had never met a better Catholic.[12]

The Hundred Years' War

The defining event in Joan's childhood was the ongoing conflict between France and England, which is now known as the Hundred Years' War. The catalyst for the war was the death of Charles IV of France—the last living male heir to the French throne—in 1328. Charles died without a son, motivating two cousins to claim they were next in line: Philip of Valois, who was Charles's first cousin through his father's brother, and Edward of Plantagenet, who was Charles's nephew through his sister.

Edward was not just any potential heir to the French throne. He was King Edward III of England, the monarch of one of the three great powers in Europe.[13] France was the wealthiest, most populous state in Western Europe. When a French court ruled against Edward's claim to the throne, he sought English control of France's rich resources by another means: war.

War began in 1337 and continued on and off for 116 years through the efforts and ambitions of Philip and Edward and their heirs, who all claimed rights to the French throne. England won the war's early battles despite its smaller size and fewer resources. Under Edward's leadership, the English military secured major victories at sea and on land, destroying the French fleet at Sluys on the Flemish coast in June 1340[14] and capturing Crecy in 1346 and Poitiers in 1356. The advantage shifted to France under the leadership of King Charles V, who regained most of his country's lost territory during his reign from 1364 to 1380. But when Charles V died and his eleven-year-old son, Charles VI, succeeded him, England, once again, reclaimed its dominance in battle.

Four of Charles VI's uncles ruled in the king's place for the first eight years of his reign. The uncles had the best interests of neither France nor their nephew at heart. The resources Charles V had built up, they squandered to finance selfish projects. Charles VI ended the regency in 1388, but his ruling authority was temporary. When he was twenty-four years old, he showed the first signs of mental illness, triggering the establishment of another regency in 1393, with his wife, Queen Isabeau of Bavaria, presiding over it.

The absence of strong leadership in France led to the outbreak of civil war between supporters of two branches of the French royal family—the Armagnacs and the Burgundians. Queen Isabeau came to align herself with the Burgundians, who were allied with England. Most of the people in Joan's town of Domrémy were French patriots who supported the Armagnacs.

King Henry V ascended to the English throne in 1413. Under his leadership, the English and Burgundians secured major victories in Agincourt in 1415 and Rouen, capital of Normandy, in January of 1419.[15] They also secured a strong and critical alliance with the twenty-three-year-old Duke of Burgundy, Philip, who inherited the dukedom when the Armagnacs murdered his father, Duke John of Burgundy, on September 10, 1419, with the knowledge, if not the actual participation, of the French Dauphin (the crown prince and future Charles VII).[16] The alliance gave England a strategic advantage because Burgundy at that time included a continuous strip of land from modern Belgium into the heart of France.[17]

In March 1420, the English and Burgundians secured another important victory at Fresnay-le-Vicomte near Le Mans, killing three thousand French soldiers and capturing their commander, Marshal Rieux.[18] In May, Queen Isabeau convinced her husband to sign a treaty between France and England that was intended to settle the century-old dispute in England's favor. The treaty, called the Treaty of Troyes, promised that Catherine, daughter of Charles VI and Isabeau, would marry Henry, and Henry would be recognized as the heir and regent of Charles VI. In June, Henry married Catherine. In December, Henry and Charles VI pronounced the Dauphin an accessory to the murder of Duke John of Burgundy and condemned him to death. In January 1421, Charles VI formally disinherited his last surviving son, the Dauphin. In December 1421, Henry and Catherine had a baby boy named for his father, who was expected to rule England as King Henry VI and France as King Henry II of France.

In 1422, the English and French monarchs—King Henry V and King Charles VI—both died. On his deathbed, Henry made his brother, John, Duke of Bedford, regent for the infant king and leader of the ongoing war effort. As historian Warren H. Carroll noted, "Under Bedford there was every reason to believe that France would be secured."[19] England's army was not merely better than France's army, it was nearly the best army in Europe, and Bedford was a formidable commander.[20]

War continued, with the English and Burgundians fighting for a united France and England, and the Armagnacs fighting for an independent France led by Charles VII, who was yet uncrowned. Under Bedford's leadership, England won decisive victories at Cravant in July 1423 and Verneuil in August 1424, nearly wiping out the French army. Carroll reflected on the seeming inevitability of an English victory: "Against all odds, and primarily as a result of the long and tragic reign of the mad King Charles VI, it appeared very likely that the smaller but more aggressive country of England would absorb the larger but beaten France, creating a united nation which by its size and power would unquestionably dominate Europe for decades or even centuries to come. It was at this point that Joan the Maid appeared upon the historical scene, and saved France."[21]

The men and women of fifteenth-century France would have seen in Joan, who called herself "la Pucelle" ("the maid," also understood to be an unmarried girl, a virgin), the fulfillment of a prophesy that had been passed down for generations: the kingdom would be lost by a woman (Isabeau of Bavaria) and saved by a virgin.

Messengers from Heaven

Joan was thirteen when she first learned God's shocking will for her life. It was the summer of 1425, around noon, and she was in her father's garden. She saw a great light coming from the direction of the village church. A voice seemed to be coming from the light. She was frightened. She heard the voice three times before knowing it was the voice of an angel.[22] This was the first of many angelic communications Joan would have during the next several years.

"This voice has always guarded me well and I have always understood it clearly," Joan said.[23]

The angel commanded her to conduct herself well and habitually go to church. Two or three times a week, it spoke of a special mission God had chosen for her: she would lead a French army to defeat the English in battle, drive the English out of France, and crown Charles VII as the rightful king.

The mission sounded ridiculous and impossible. Why would God choose a simple farm girl to do the work of an experienced military leader? Joan knew nothing about combat or military strategy. Why would French noblemen entrust her with command of an army? How would she convince soldiers to obey her? How would she know what to do at any point along the way in this absurd-sounding plan?

Confused, Joan objected, explaining to the angel that she did not know how to ride a horse or lead an army in battle. But the heavenly messenger was adamant about God's plan for her life. And because nothing is impossible for God,[24] she listened.

The angel gave her specific instructions. She was to leave home without telling her father and make her way to Robert de Baudricourt in the fortress of Vaucouleurs. Baudricourt would give her an army to command. She would lead soldiers into the city of Orléans and drive the English out.

What the angel told her was too outlandish to be true. But it was true. And Joan knew it was true. "St. Michael assured me of it before the voices came," she explained.

SAINTLY INSPIRATION:
SAINT MICHAEL THE ARCHANGEL

Saint Michael, whose name means, "Who is like unto God," has been honored as the commander of God's army and protector of the Church since the time of the apostles.[25] Known as the first Christian and first defender of the kingship of God, he has been by God's side since the beginning of creation. He plays a crucial role in the divine plan for the salvation of the world.

Saint Michael is an angel, which means he is an intelligent, purely spiritual being who was created to love and serve God for eternity in heaven. He surpasses in glory and power all the other heavenly hosts. Like all angels, he has a distinct personality and vocation—and he exercises free will to do God's will.

God is the good and loving King of the Universe. He is not a tyrant who rules by force. He gives His subjects the choice to obey His commands because He loves freedom.

Freedom, according to the *Catechism of the Catholic Church*, is "the power, rooted in reason and will, to act or not to act, to do this or that, and so to perform deliberate actions on one's own responsibility," such that the more one does what is good and just, the freer one becomes.[26] Freedom is a beautiful gift that can be abused. Choosing evil makes one less free because it makes sin the master of the will.[27]

According to Venerable Mary of Agreda, who wrote a history of the creation of the world based on revelations given to her by the Blessed Virgin Mary, in the beginning, God created the angels without fully admitting them to the unveiled vision of His glory. He placed them under probation in heaven, giving them the opportunity to merit their consummate destiny through acts of free will. Accordingly, He initiated a trial of obedience by revealing three truths of His saving plan for creation.[28]

First, He revealed the truth of His nature: that He is "God, one in substance, triune in person . . . their Creator and Highest Lord, infinite in His essence and attributes." He commanded the angels to adore and revere Him. All obeyed, but not in the same way. Saint Michael and the other good and holy angels obeyed joyfully, reciprocating God's love out of a desire to do justice, and freely admitting and believing what was above their intelligence. An angel named Lucifer, however, obeyed with imperfect charity and a divided will. Wanting of love, he put himself in danger of falling.[29]

Second, according to the revelations of Venerable Mary of Agreda, God revealed His design for humans: that He would create reasoning beings who would be lower than angels, who would nonetheless stand in high favor with Him. Humans would share the same purpose as angels of loving and serving their Creator—and the second Person of the Blessed Trinity would become incarnate, such that all angels and humans would serve Him, acknowledging and adoring His fully human, fully divine nature.[30]

Third, He revealed that the woman who would form the incarnate God in her womb would be queen of heaven and earth, to be honored by all angels and humans.[31]

Again, Michael and the good and holy angels humbly and lovingly acknowledged and embraced God's will. But Lucifer was overcome with pride and envy. Refusing to accept his inferiority to any human—and especially the fully human mother of the incarnate God—he resisted. He imagined an alternative world order, independent and separate from Christ, where he would be the head of the human race and all angelic orders. He decided to rebel and persuaded innumerable angels to follow him as their leader.[32] He told their Creator, "Unjust are these commands and injury is done to my greatness; this human nature which Thou, Lord, lookest upon with so much love and which thou favorest so highly, I will persecute and destroy. To this end I will direct all my power and all my aspirations. And this Woman, Mother of the Word, I will hurl from the position in which Thou hast proposed to place her, and at my hands, the plan which Thou settest up, shall come to be naught."[33]

The Lord responded, "This Woman, whom thou refusest to honor, shall crush thy head and by her shalt thou be vanquished and annihilated (Gen 3:15). And if, through thy pride, death enters the world (Wis. 2:24), life and salvation of mortals shall enter through the humility of this Woman. Those that are of the nature and likeness of that Man and Woman, shall enjoy the gifts and the crowns, which thou and thy followers have lost."[34]

He showed them an image of the Blessed Virgin Mary, the perfect and beautiful woman who would be their queen.[35] The good angels, led by Saint Michael, responded by praising her and defending her honor. The bad angels, led by Lucifer, responded with hatred and fury, refusing to accept their inferiority to a mortal woman. Threatening destruction of the whole human race, they initiated the heavenly conflict described in Revelation: "Now war arose in heaven, Michael and his angels fighting against the dragon; and the dragon and his angels fought, but they were defeated and there was no longer any place for them in heaven. And the great dragon was thrown down, that ancient serpent, who is called the Devil and Satan, the deceiver of the whole world—he was thrown down to the earth, and his angels were thrown down with him" (Rv 12:7–9).

The defeat of Lucifer's army restored the eschatological glory of heaven to a blessed community of all who are perfectly incorporated into Christ. Since then, heaven's angels joyfully serve as messengers of His saving plan, relying on wills that correspond to the Will of their Creator.

As God's highest-ranking and most trusted angel, Saint Michael executes the divine plan in mysterious and powerful ways. His offices and responsibilities include Defender of God's People, Protector of the Church, Helper and Defender of Christians, Advocate of the Dying, Consoler of Poor Souls, and Guardian of the Blessed Sacrament and of the Pope, among others.

Holy Scripture records Saint Michael's assistance to God's people from the time of Adam and Eve to the end times in the New Testament, identifying him by name five times as "the archangel Michael,"[36] "Michael, the great prince,"[37] "Michael, one of the chief princes,"[38] "Michael, your prince,"[39] and "Michael and his angels."[40] Christian tradition holds that it was Saint Michael who assisted the armies of Israel in the battles mentioned in the Old Testament, for example at the siege at Jericho (see Jo 5:13–15) and the defeat of the Assyrians at the attempted siege of Jerusalem (see 2 Kgs 19:32–35). The Fathers of the Church speculate that it was Saint Michael who led Adam into the Garden of Eden and stood guard at the gate of paradise with flaming sword "to keep the way of the tree of life," warned Noah of the coming flood, informed Abraham that he was the father of the chosen people, appeared to Moses in the burning bush, assisted the Israelites in their departure from Egypt, and gave the Ten Commandments to the Israelites on Mount Sinai.[41] In addition, it was Saint Michael or the soldiers under his command who assisted Jesus—whose power is infinite and exceeds that of all creatures—when He was tempted by Satan in the desert and again when He awaited His betrayal in the Garden of Gethsemane (see Mt 4:11; Lk 22:43). Finally, it will be Saint Michael who defeats Satan and his demons in the final battle at the end of the world (see Rv 12:10).

Saint Michael has served as the Church's fierce and constant guardian since her founding on Good Friday and Pentecost. Although he usually assists in ways that are unseen by humans, on a few occasions involving critical moments for the Church, he has made his presence known.

The victory of Constantine the Great over Emperor Maxentius at the Battle of the Milvian Bridge in 312 is one of those moments. At the time, Constantine was not a Christian, but he credited the Christian God with his swift victory because he obeyed a command that had been given to him in a vision and dream to honor Christ in battle. Constantine's triumph marked the end of the Roman persecution of Christians and the beginning of Christendom. As sole emperor of Rome from 312 to 337, Constantine spread Christianity throughout the empire and beyond: he founded

Constantinople as a Christian city, promoted Christians to high ranks in the government and military, and presided over the First Council of Nicaea. He also built churches in Rome (including the original Saint Peter's Basilica), the Holy Land (including the Church of the Nativity in Bethlehem and the Church of the Holy Sepulcher in Jerusalem), and Constantinople. In the ancient town of Thrace, which was north of Constantinople, he built a magnificent church called the Michaelion in honor of Saint Michael. Upon completion of the Michaelion, the commander in chief of the heavenly hosts appeared to Constantine, saying, "I am Michael, the chief of the angelic legions of the Lord of hosts, the protector of the Christian Religion, who while you were battling against godless tyrants, placed the weapons in your hands."[42] Constantine was baptized a Christian before he died.[43]

Devotion to Saint Michael has been a constant practice of Christians throughout the ages. It was especially strong in medieval France, where Saint Michael was the patron of the French royal family and soldiers fighting against faithless armies. Many French sites were named after Saint Michael, including at least forty-six churches in Joan's neighboring dioceses.[44]

Saint Michael's feast day is September 29. He is the patron saint of soldiers, the military, police officers, security guards, physicians, paramedics, radiologists, emergency medical technicians (EMTs), sick people, and sailors. He is also the patron of a holy death and against temptations.

A prayer to Saint Michael, which was written by Pope Leo XIII in 1886 and is prayed daily by many Christians today, especially after Mass, reveals the Church's great reliance on her most powerful angelic intercessor:

> Saint Michael the Archangel,
> defend us in battle.
> Be our protection against the wickedness and
>   snares of the devil.
> May God rebuke him, we humbly pray;
> and do Thou, O prince of the heavenly hosts,
> by the Power of God,
> cast into hell Satan and all the evil spirits
> who prowl throughout the world seeking the
>   ruin of souls. Amen.

The Divine Counsel of Saint Michael

Joan's first encounter with Saint Michael was a frightening experience. She never expected to be visited by a heavenly being, much less the prince of the heavenly hosts. She did not recognize her visitor at first because she could not make sense of what was happening to her. But with each meeting, Saint Michael shared more details about God's astounding plan for her life. His words revealed his absolute devotion to the Creator. She soon realized that the spiritual being counseling her to help the king of France was the first defender of the kingship of Christ.

Saint Michael, whose will is perfectly united to God's will, provided advice and inspiration to Joan. Before all else, Saint Michael told her to be a good child and that God would help her. He said that she would receive further guidance from Saint Catherine and Saint Margaret, who would come to her. He instructed her to believe them.

Saintly Inspiration:
Saint Margaret of Antioch

According to legend, Margaret lived in Antioch during the reign of the Roman emperor Diocletian between 284 and 305.[45] Antioch was an ancient city in the Roman Empire, located along the Orontes River in modern-day Turkey. The city played an important role in the early days of the Church. As recorded in the Acts of the Apostles:

> And the hand of the Lord was with them, and a great number that believed turned to the Lord. News of this came to the ears of the church in Jerusalem, and they sent Barnabas to Antioch. When he came and saw the grace of God, he was glad; and he exhorted them all to remain faithful to the Lord with stead-fast purpose; for he was a good man, full of the Holy Spirit and of faith. And a large company was added to the Lord. So Barnabas went to Tarsus to look for Saul; and when he had found him, he brought him to Antioch. For a whole year they met with the church, and taught a large company of people; and in Antioch the disciples were for the first time called Christians. (Acts 11:21–26)

Eusebius, the fourth-century bishop of Caesarea who is considered the first historian of Christianity, recorded that Christians in the Roman Empire lived peacefully, and

Christianity flourished, during most of Diocletian's reign. He observed that people flocked to Christianity as magnificent churches were built and Church leaders "were courted and honored with the greatest subserviency by all the rulers and governors."[46]

In 302, the Roman response to Christianity changed overnight when Diocletian resolved to suppress the Faith at a council at Nicodemia.[47] Over the next few years, he presided over the most severe persecutions of the early Church,[48] ordering the seizure of Church assets, destruction of Christian churches, burning of scriptures, and imprisonment and torture of bishops and priests. In 303, he offered amnesty to imprisoned clerics, ordering that they be set free if they apostatized and made a sacrifice to the pagan gods. In 304, Diocletian ordered that all people, in all cities, be gathered in a public space to make an offering to the pagan gods— and all men, women, and children who refused be executed.

Margaret of Antioch grew up amidst Diocletian's persecution. Also known as Marina, she was the beautiful daughter of a pagan priest. She knew her father expected her to adopt his beliefs, but she learned about Christianity and came to believe that Jesus Christ was her Savior. Without telling her father, she became a Christian and took a vow of virginity. When her father found out about her conversion, he ordered the teenaged Margaret to leave his home.

Margaret became a shepherdess and continued to live as a Christian. One day when she was tending sheep, a prefect of the Roman Empire named Olybrius noticed her. He became infatuated with her beauty and tried to seduce her. When she refused him, he became angry and charged her with being a Christian. He had her tortured and imprisoned.

While in prison, the devil came to her in the form of a dragon. He swallowed her but did not kill her, because she was holding the ultimate weapon: a cross. She set herself free by scratching the cross against his throat, causing him to disgorge her.[49]

The next day, the officers attempted to execute her by setting her on fire and drowning her in water. She miraculously survived, converting thousands of amazed spectators on the spot. In anger, the officers immediately executed all the new Christians.[50] They beheaded Margaret, who died a martyr, joining Saint Peter, Saint Barnabas, and the other saints of the early Church who would spend eternity with Jesus in heaven.

No written records exist about Saint Margaret, but the early Christians preserved her story—most likely embellishing it through the years—as a part of the Christian tradition. Devotion to Saint Margaret was widespread in medieval Europe. The people of Domrémy had a special devotion to her, and Joan's parish church was home to a statue of her.[51]

She is a special patroness of falsely accused people.[52] Her feast day is July 20.

SAINTLY INSPIRATION:
SAINT CATHERINE OF ALEXANDRIA

According to tradition, Catherine was born in Alexandria, Egypt in the late third century. Founded by Alexander the Great in 331 BC and transformed into a Roman province by

Octavian, the future Caesar Augustus, in 30 BC, Alexandria was the intellectual and commercial metropolis of the world for centuries.[53] The city played an important role in the early Christian Church. Saint Mark the Evangelist, the author of the Gospel of Mark, brought Christianity to Alexandria in AD 49 after traveling with Saint Peter and writing down his sermons. He became the first bishop of Alexandria—a post that held great significance in the Church for centuries when the bishop of Alexandria was second only to the bishop of Rome.

Catherine came of age during the Diocletian persecution, the last and most horrific Roman persecution of Christians that took place between 303 and 312.[54] The historian Eusebius, who witnessed some of the Egyptian martyrdoms, recorded:

> The outrages and sufferings which the martyrs in the Thebais endured surpass all description, their whole bodies being torn to pieces by shells instead of claws even until life was gone; and women were tied by one foot and were raised on high through the air, head downwards, by certain machines, with their bodies completely naked and without even a covering, and they furnished this most shameful and cruel and inhuman sight of all to all the onlookers; and others again died on being fastened to tree trunks and stumps; for having brought together the very strongest of the branches by certain machines, and stretching the legs of the martyrs one by one on each of these, they released the branches to be carried back to their

natural position, planning a sudden separation of the
limbs of those against whom they devised this.

And all these things, indeed, were carried out not
for a few days or a short time, but for a long interval of
entire years, sometimes of more than ten, sometimes
more than twenty in number being destroyed, sometimes not less than thirty and then again nearly sixty;
and again at other times one hundred men in a single
day, together with very young children and women
were slain.[55]

Several emperors governed the empire during this time of
heightened Christian persecution. Some were enthusiastic
torturers and killers of Christians. Others were "strictly men
of the moment, men of the sword, incapable of imagining
any goal and purpose for their lives beyond power for themselves." One of these "men of the moment" was Emperor
Maxentius. He was relatively neutral toward Christianity
but his reign was marked by "flagrant immorality and arbi-
trary tyranny."[56] He played an important role in the account
of Saint Catherine's life that Christians have preserved for
more than 1,700 years.

Catherine was a beautiful and intelligent girl who was
born to a noble family. Her father may have been Cons-
tus, the governor of Alexandria.[57] He gave her an education,
exposing her to philosophy and theology at a young age. She
excelled in her studies. At the age of fourteen, she became
a Christian after having a vision of Mother Mary and the
infant Jesus.

When Catherine was eighteen, Emperor Maxentius hosted a pagan festival on a visit to Alexandria. He threatened to kill Christians who refused to join in the festivities by offering sacrifices to the gods against their will.

Catherine was not a target of the persecutions, but she was deeply upset about them. She went to see Emperor Maxentius. She denounced his cruelty, and as they argued, Maxentius was too captivated by Catherine's beauty and intellect to kill her. He wanted to win her over by convincing her to abandon her beliefs. He summoned fifty philosophers to debate her, but instead of convincing her, she convinced them with her passionate defense of truth. They converted to Christianity and Maxentius burned them to death.

In anger, Maxentius had Catherine arrested and scourged. She remained strong in her faith, refusing to denounce her Savior who had reserved a place for her in heaven. Amazed and deeply moved, Maxentius's wife, an officer, and two hundred soldiers on her guard converted to Christianity. Maxentius had them all killed.[58]

Maxentius tried another tactic. He proposed marriage, offering to make her a powerful empress. She refused, saying she had dedicated her virginity to Jesus Christ, her spouse.

Finally, he sentenced Catherine to a torturous death reserved for the worst criminals: execution on a breaking wheel. This was a special form of torture, requiring an executioner to thread a person's limbs through the spokes of a wheel, strike them with a heavy rod, and break their bones, causing a slow and painful death.[59]

When the officers presented the wheel to Catherine, she touched it and it miraculously shattered. Maxentius had her beheaded, sending her soul to her eternal home in heaven with her spouse, Jesus Christ.

Saint Catherine was one of the most beloved saints of medieval Europe. Nearly all churches were home to a statue of her, and many churches were named after her, including a church near Domrémy in Maxey. In France, her feast day, November 25, was a holy day of obligation where work was prohibited and families were expected to gather in worship.[60]

Saint Catherine is the patroness of philosophers, maidens, and preachers.

Joan Leaves Home for the First Time

For three years, Joan appeared to live a normal life at home. She helped her parents, went to Mass, spent time with friends and family, and prayed. All the while, her heavenly messengers provided spiritual guidance and greater clarity about her mission. Saint Margaret's example may have been particularly helpful to Joan at this time as she contemplated taking the first daunting step in her journey—leaving home. Saint Margaret was a teenager when she was forced to leave her home to live her faith out in the world, alone.

In May 1428, when Joan was sixteen years old, she knew the time had come to go to Baudricourt in the fortress of Vaucouleurs. She needed a reason to leave home that would not only satisfy her parents but also put her in position to speak with Baudricourt. Providentially, her mother's cousin, Jeanne Laxart, was expecting a baby. Jeanne and her husband, Durand, lived in the village of Burey-le-Petit, near Vaucouleurs.

Joan went to stay with Jeanne and Durand. While at their home, she helped with housework, spinning, gardening, and looking after the animals. After she built up trust with her hosts, she asked Durand to escort her to Vaucouleurs, and he agreed.

Joan and Durand journeyed to Vaucouleurs and were granted an audience with Baudricourt. She told him she had come on behalf of the Lord, who wanted him to give her an army to command. She asked Baudricourt to tell the king to have patience and not attack his enemies because the Lord would send help. She added "most emphatically," according to an aristocrat who was present at the meeting, that "the Kingdom of France did not belong to the Dauphin but to the Lord, who had given the country into the king's trust." Baudricourt asked Joan who this "Lord" was to whom she was referring. "The King of Heaven," she replied.

Baudricourt thought the idea of God sending him a girl to command an army was ridiculous. He told Durand to give Joan a sound whipping and send her back to her father.

Joan Keeps a Vow of Chastity

Joan returned from Vaucouleurs unsuccessful but undeterred. Trusting that God would provide the help she needed, she reengaged in her old life, but was more contemplative and prayerful than she had been before she left. At least one friend speculated that the change in her personality meant she expected to marry soon. This was a reasonable assumption. Most girls at that time were engaged by the time they were twelve or thirteen years old and married soon thereafter.[61] Joan, however, was not like most girls. When the angel first came to her when she was thirteen years old, she gave herself completely to God, promising to be chaste "for as long as it should please [Him]."[62] Similar to Saint Margaret, she kept her vow between her and God, telling neither her mother nor her father.

Joan's secret was a burden because she knew that her parents expected her to marry. When she was sixteen years old, they arranged a marriage for her. She refused to go along with it and her suitor refused to accept her refusal. Attempting to enforce the promise against her will, he had her summoned to appear before a judge in a court of justice in the city of Toul. She went to court and told the judge the truth—that she had never made a promise to marry—and she prevailed.[63] The local bishop dismissed the case in Joan's favor because the sacrament of Matrimony is invalid without the consent of both the man and woman.[64]

This was the only time Joan could recall disobeying her parents, but it was not the only time she would choose God's will over theirs.

The War Comes to Joan

While Joan was defending against an unwanted marriage, war intensified between the Armagnacs, who supported the French Valois royal family, and the Burgundians, who were allied with England. In July 1428, the Burgundians attacked and pillaged the towns surrounding Domrémy.[65] "For fear of the Burgundians," Joan's family fled to the town of Neufchâteau in Lorraine, where they stayed at the small inn owned by a woman called La Rousse for about fifteen days.[66] Joan and her mother helped with household chores during their stay. When they returned to Domrémy, they were deeply upset to find that their local church, among other buildings, had been plundered and burned, and women who had stayed behind had been attacked.[67]

In October, the residents of Domrémy heard the distressing news that the English were making swift progress against the Armagnacs: they had invaded Orléans, the last major city loyal to the Valois, and destroyed the bridge leading to King Charles VII in Chinon. The English planned to cut off Orléans's food and other supplies.[68]

After Christmas, Joan left home without telling anyone. She explained, "Since God commanded it, it had to be. Since God commanded it, had I had a hundred fathers and a hundred mothers, had I been a King's daughter, I should have departed."[69]

She walked ten miles to Vaucouleurs and stayed with friends of Jeanne and Durand Laxart, the Le Royers.[70] Then, once again, she requested an audience with Baudricourt, whom her heavenly messengers had assured her would assist her in fulfilling her mission.

Baudricourt granted her an audience—and this time, he listened. His advisors ridiculed Joan, but he made up his own mind about her. He was moved by her passion for helping King Charles become recognized as the one, true king of France. However, he refused to send her to see Charles. Undeterred, Joan stayed in Vaucouleurs and went to daily Mass as she awaited the work of the Holy Spirit.

Jean le Fumeux, parish priest of Ugny who served as

churchwarden of the chapel Notre Dame of Vaucouleurs, observed Joan at church during this time. He recalled, "I often saw Joan the Maid come to that church very piously. She heard Mass in the morning and remained long at prayer. I have seen her beneath the vault of that church on her knees before the Holy Virgin, sometimes with bowed head, sometimes with her head raised."[71]

At the end of January of 1429, Baudricourt decided to test Joan. He summoned her to travel to the town of Nancy in Lorraine, where she was to meet the father-in-law of his good friend—Charles, Duke of Lorraine—who was sixty-four years old and in poor health. Durand Laxard accompanied her on her journey, along with one or two of Baudricourt's squires. Joan was asked to perform a miracle to cure Charles of his ailing health. Joan obliged, but not in the way that was expected. She told him she had no control over his physical health, and she advised him to give up his mistress, take back his wife, and pray to God for restoration of his physical health. Charles was not cured of his physical ailments, but he was impressed. He gave Joan money for her journey.[72]

On February 12, upon her return to Vaucouleurs, she told Baudricourt that the English had defeated the French in battle that day. A few days later, news arrived to Baudricourt confirming that the French army did in fact suffer a crushing defeat on February 12; the English had intercepted a French supply convoy in Rouvray, just north of Orléans, coming from Paris that consisted of "some 300 carts and wagons, carrying crossbow shafts, cannons and cannonballs but also barrels of herring."[73]

Baudricourt decided to grant Joan's request to send her with an escort to meet the king. He arranged a meeting for her with his loyal companion, Jean de Metz, who would lead the escort. Metz questioned Joan about her urgent need to see the king and was struck by her answer. She told him, "There is nobody in all the world, neither king nor duke, nor daughter of the King of Scotland, nor any other who can recover the kingdom for France. And there will be no help (for the kingdom) if not for me. Although I would rather have remained spinning at my mother's side, for it is not my condition, yet must I go and must I do this thing, for my Lord wills that I do so."[74]

So moved was Metz by Joan's sincerity that he put his hand in hers and promised to lead her to the king. He asked when she wanted to leave and she said, "Rather today than tomorrow and tomorrow rather than later."[75] He asked if she wanted to go in her own clothes, and realizing that she could not ride hundreds of miles wearing her house skirt, she answered that she would rather have a man's riding outfit. He gave her some of his servant's clothing and arranged for the king's supporters in Vaucouleurs to make men's clothes and shoes and provide a horse for her.[76]

Joan was ready for her journey to Chinon. Her host in Vaucouleurs, Henri Le Royer, recalled a conversation with her soon before she departed. He recalled, "When she sought to go, she was asked how she would do it, when there were so many men-at-arms everywhere. She answered that she feared not men-at arms for her way was open, and if there were men-at-arms on her road, she had God, her Lord, who would clear the way for her to go to the lord Dauphin, and that she had been born to do this."[77]

At seventeen years old, with the help, support, and inspiration of Saint Michael, Saint Catherine, and Saint Margaret, and with danger "everywhere," she embraced the unique role God had chosen for her in this world—and she was unafraid.

Journey to Chinon

Dressed in men's clothing and armed with a sword Baudricourt had given her, Joan was finally on her way to Chinon to meet the king. Her escorts included two noblemen—Metz and Bertrand de Poulengy, the king's attorney—and three servants. On Baudricourt's order, the men swore to lead Joan "truly and surely" on her 350-mile journey.[78]

Of course, Joan also had the guidance of her heavenly messengers who accompanied her on the journey. And no wonder. The roads out of Vaucouleurs were not safe from Burgundian and English soldiers. Metz recalled that the enemy was "everywhere."[79] For protection, the group traveled under the cover of night. Along the way, Joan noted that it would be good, but not wise, to go to Mass because it would put them at risk of being detected by the enemy. They did receive the graces from Mass twice on their journey, however, when they traveled through the town of Auxerre and Saint-Catherine-de-Fierbois.[80]

The journey took eleven days, and during that time, the men often expressed their fear and anxiety. Joan repeatedly told them not to be afraid. She told them that as soon as they arrived at Chinon, the king would welcome them.

The men accompanying Joan did not expect her sanctity to penetrate their hearts. In fact, despite their promise to Baudricourt, some of them left Vaucouleurs with dishonorable intentions against her chastity. But Joan had an astonishing influence over them. They recognized an "abundance of goodness" in her.[81] They saw that she never swore and never saw any evil in her. De Poulengy recalled, "It seemed to me that she was sent by God . . . [that she] was so virtuous a girl that she seemed a saint."[82] Metz shared a similar thought: "I believe that she was sent by God."[83]

On Thursday, March 3, they stopped in Saint-Catherine-de-Fierbois, a village ten miles east of Chinon. The village was named for Saint Catherine of Alexandria, the teenaged martyr known for her courageous and persuasive words and actions, who had been communicating with Joan from heaven. They went to Mass and ate a meal. Joan dictated two letters there: one to her parents, asking for forgiveness for her departure, and the other to the king, seeking permission to enter Chinon.[84]

On Friday, March 4, they arrived in Chinon. Two royal counselors interrogated Joan. One did not believe her fantastic claims, but the other did; he believed that she had been sent by God and he advised the king to see her.[85] At the same time, the king received a letter from Baudricourt confirming that the people of Vaucouleurs had found her to be pious and brave.

On Sunday, March 6, nearly four years after being informed that she was destined to restore the French crown to the rightful heir, she was granted an audience with the true and rightful king.[86]

Meeting the Rightful King

As Joan and her escorts arrived at the castle at Chinon, a man on horseback approached them. "Isn't this the famous maid from Vaucouleurs?" he asked.[87] "If I could have you for one night, you wouldn't be a maiden anymore!" he said lewdly.[88] She scolded him for disrespecting her virtue and warned him that he was near death. He died within the hour.

Joan was led into the Great Hall, where a test awaited her. The room was filled with more than three hundred courtiers and supporters of the Armagnacs; the king was among them, but he was dressed in ordinary attire to conceal his identity. Joan identified him at once.[89] Without expressing a moment of confusion or hesitation, Joan approached the handsome, plain-dressed, twenty-six-year-old king and said, "My most eminent lord Dauphin, I have come, sent by God, to bring help to you and to the kingdom."[90]

Charles asked her name and she replied, "Gentle Dauphin, Joan the Maid is my name, and to you is sent word by me from the King of Heaven that you will be anointed and crowned in the town of Reims and you will be Lieutenant to the King of Heaven who is King of France. . . . I tell thee, on behalf of Messire, that thou art true heir of France and King's son, and He has sent me to thee to lead thee to Reims, that thou mayst receive thy coronation and thy consecration, if thou wilt."[91]

Joan and Charles met privately. She revealed to him a secret known only to him and God—and it transformed him.[92] For years, the king had been burdened by the war, his disinheritance, and the assassination of the Duke of Burgundy. Anxiety and hopelessness had defined his days and shaped his demeanor; he was known for his indecisiveness and lack of fervor. When he appeared from his meeting with Joan, he looked uncharacteristically radiant.[93]

Joan's Fair Duke

Jean the Duke of Alençon was twenty-three years old when he first heard about Joan the Maid. It was the spring of 1429, just two weeks after he had been released as a prisoner of war. Alençon came from a long line of soldiers who had fought valiantly to defend France against English aggressors. His great-grandfather, grandfather, and father had all fought for France, with his great-grandfather and father giving their lives at the Battles of Crecy and Agincourt, respectively. Alençon was a teenager when he began his military career. He was seventeen years old when he was captured at the Battle of Verneuil in 1424, spending five years in captivity until his wife purchased his freedom with an enormous ransom.[94]

England had made significant gains in the war during his imprisonment. English troops and their allies now controlled most of Northern France and were heading south with the goal of capturing Orléans. They were well on their way. Having established garrisons to the north and west of Orléans, they concentrated soldiers in the south and forced French troops to retreat into the city. The loss of Orléans seemed inevitable—so much so that key military leaders refused to support efforts to fortify the city.[95]

When Alençon heard that Charles had received at court a young woman claiming to be sent by God to raise the siege on Orléans, he was intrigued. Charles was more than his king; he was his close friend and father to his godson. He rode to Chinon at once. On March 7, he arrived at the castle and found Joan and Charles in conversation. When Joan found out who he was, she said to him, "The more people we have who share the blood of France, the better it will be."[96] He and Joan became fast friends. They dined together with Charles the next day, and after their meal, they jousted with each other. "Seeing her manage her lance so well, I gave her a horse," he recalled.[97]

Alençon would become Joan's greatest friend and ally in the army; she would affectionately call him "my fair Duke."

An Interrogation and a Peace Offering

Charles wanted to believe that Joan was sent by God to save France. He also wanted churchmen and intellectuals to confirm her claims. He subjected Joan to two days of interrogations in Chinon by bishops and priests, followed by a two-week period of intense interrogations in Poitiers, thirty miles away, by two bishops, the confessors of the king and queen, and several renowned theologians of the Universities of Paris and Orléans.[98] Joan answered all questions truthfully, exhibiting her complete trust in God and His ways. But she grew impatient as the days went on. When she was asked for a sign to prove her directive from God, she replied,

"In the name of God: I did not come to Poitiers to produce signs. Lead me to Orléans, and I will show you the sign."[99]

Satisfied by Joan's sincerity and audacity, the interrogators gave their recommendation to the king, reporting, "In her is found no evil, but only good, humility, virginity, devotion, honesty, simplicity. Now seeing that the king finds no evil in her either, and aware of her urgent request to be sent to Orléans—to show that indeed she is the bearer of divine aid—the king should not hinder her from going to Orléans with soldiers. Rather, he should send her there forthwith, trusting God. To fear or reject her would be to rebel against the Holy Spirit and to render oneself unworthy of divine aid."[100]

On the Tuesday of Holy Week, March 22, 1429, Joan dictated a peace offering to the English, warning them that the "French shall do [to them] the greatest feat of arms which ever was done for Christianity" if they refused to leave France. The letter stated:

> ✚Jesus Maria✚
>
> King of England, and you Duke of Bedford, who call yourself regent of France. . . . Render to the Maid here sent by God the King of Heaven, the keys of all the good towns which you have taken and violated in France. She is here to make peace, if you will acknowledge her to be right, provided that France you render, and pay for having held it. And you, archers, companions of war, men-at-arms and others who are before the town of Orléans, go away into your country, by God. And if so be not done, expect news of the Maid

who will come to see you shortly, to your very great injury.

King of England, if you do not do so, I am chief-of-war and in whatever place I attain your people in France, I will make them quit it. And if they will not obey, I will have them all slain; I am here sent by God, the King of Heaven, Son of St. Mary, but will hold it for King Charles, the rightful heir, for God, King of Heaven so wills it, and that is revealed to him by the Maid who will enter into Paris with a goodly company. If you will not believe the news conveyed by God and the Maid, in what place soever we find you, we shall strike into it. . . . And believe firmly that the King of Heaven will send greater strength to the Maid than you will be able to bring up against her and her good men-at-arms and when it comes to blows will it be seen who has the better right of the God of Heaven.

You, Duke of Bedford, the Maid prays and requires of you that you cause no more destruction to be done. If you grant her right, still may you come into her company there where the French shall do the greatest feat of arms which ever was done for Christianity. And make answer if you wish to make peace in the city of Orléans. And if you make it not, you shall shortly remember it, to your very great injury.[101]

Joan had known God's will for France and England for nearly four years. Now the leaders of both countries knew it too. It was up to them to obey.

Joan Becomes a Soldier

Joan had obtained the recommendation of noble advisors, the friendship of a fair duke, and the blessing of the indecisive king. It was time for the teenage girl to follow in Saint Michael's footsteps and become the commander of God's army in France. The king's men provided Joan with a full suit of armor, an ancient sword that they recovered at Saint-Catherine-de-Fierbois per her instructions, and a staff of men fitting for a high-ranking military officer. Her staff included a squire, two pages, two pursuivants (messengers with special immunity, per the chivalric code), and two chaplains.

Inspired by Saint Margaret and Saint Catherine, who instructed her to "boldly" carry a banner honoring Christ into battle, Joan commissioned a Scottish artist to create a standard and pennon (pennant); Joan would carry the standard to give the troops a clear location to rally around in the chaos of battle, and her squire would carry the pennon to mark her position on the battlefield. Both banners would include a cherished symbol of France—lilies. Joan's standard was a magnificent three feet high by twelve feet long. In her own words, "The field of it was sown with lilies, and therein was our Lord holding the world, with two angels, one on either hand. It was white, and on it there were written the names Jesus Maria, and it was fringed with silk."[102] Joan said she loved her standard "forty times better than [her] sword."[103]

The pennon was much smaller than the standard and triangular in shape. It depicted the scene of the Annunciation—the Archangel Gabriel's declaration to Mary that she would conceive and bear the Son of God in her womb—with

Gabriel presenting Mary with a double lily rather than the infant Jesus. Fr. Jean Pasquerel created a third banner depicting the scene of the crucifixion with the words, "Jesus Crucified." He and the other priests used it to gather the army for daily prayer and devotion.

On April 21, Joan went to the town of Blois to join the soldiers who were stationed there. To prepare them to fight as Christians, she demanded that they behave virtuously: they would avoid foul language, not engage with prostitutes, and honor God throughout the day. As her squire, Jean d'Aulon, recalled, "Twice a day, morning and evening, she assembled the priests, with whom she sang anthems and hymns, and she invited the soldiers to go to one of them for private confession."[104] In just a few days, the soldiers developed great confidence in her ability to lead them to victory.

On April 27, Joan marched to Orléans with her army and Alençon, their commander. Led by Fr. Jean Pasquerel and other clergy members, they marched for two days behind the banner of the crucifixion: it was a reminder that the King of the Universe had experienced human suffering in pursuit of the divine will.

Raising the Siege on Orléans

The situation in Orléans had been desperate for months. The crisis began on October 12, 1428, when five thousand English soldiers arrived in the city and seized the fortified bridge across the Loire twelve days later.[105] While the English did not have enough troops to invade the city completely, they made effective use of their manpower, taking control of all but one entrance gate and constructing garrisons in strategic locations designed to cut off French supplies. By early 1429, the people were starving.[106] While many French military leaders wanted to give up, the people wanted to fight; they yearned for a leader who shared their patriotism and belief that right would triumph.[107]

Nearly two hundred days after the English arrived in Orléans, that leader was on her way. News of the maid who had been sent by God to defeat the English had reached the people of Orléans—and they were overjoyed.

On Friday, April 29, Joan and her army arrived in Checy, five miles from the eastern Bourgoyne Gate—the only entrance that was unguarded by the English.[108] Jean de Dunois, the French military leader stationed in New Orléans, greeted them and told Joan that "many were longing" for her at the other side of the Loire River. He convinced her that their first duty was getting the provisions that her army had brought with them to the city. As such, they loaded the convoy onto the boats. But they encountered a great difficulty: the stream and wind were going in the opposite direction.

Joan told him, "This succor does not come from me, but from God Himself, Who . . . has had compassion on the town of Orléans." At that moment, "the wind, being contrary, and thereby preventing the boats going up the river . . . turned all at once and became favorable" and the supplies were delivered.[109] From that moment, Dunois had "good hope" in the maid who had already won the confidence of the people. He implored her to cross the Loire to meet the patriots who eagerly awaited her arrival.[110]

It was 8:00 p.m. when Joan rode into Orléans. Wearing full armor, carrying her battle standard, and riding a white horse, she was greeted by a "marvelous crowd" of French loyalists.[111] Over the next few days, French supplies and reinforcements arrived in Orléans, and the army grew to four thousand soldiers. Meanwhile, Joan spent time with the people of Orléans. She showed kindness to the men, women, and children who flooded the streets to be in her presence, and they "felt themselves already comforted and as if no longer besieged."[112]

Joan saw battle for the first time on Wednesday, five days after she arrived in Orléans. She was napping when her heavenly messengers alerted her that it was time to fight. She mounted her horse and led the French in a surprise attack of Fort St. Loup. The French killed three quarters of the garrison's soldiers in a swift victory.[113] Joan wept at the sight of the dead bodies whom she knew had died without confession. She prayed for their souls. Back at camp, she instructed Father Pasquerel to order the French soldiers to give thanks to God for their victory and confess their sins, noting that she would leave them if they refused.[114]

The following day, Thursday, was the solemnity of the Ascension of Christ into heaven. In observance of the holy day, the soldiers did not fight. Joan rose early the next morning, confessed to Father Pasquerel, and heard Mass with her men. Then she participated in a war council, giving a strategy recommendation for battle the next day that put her strongly at odds with Dunois. She refused to back down and her plan was accepted by the rest of the council. That afternoon, she wrote a letter to the English ordering them to leave France on the orders of the King of heaven. She tied the letter to an arrow and instructed an archer to deliver it by shooting it to the English. Not expecting her soldiers to be spared bloodshed, she commanded that "no man should dare on the morrow go out of the city to assault or attack if he had not first been to confession."[115] That evening, she told Father Pasquerel that she would be wounded in battle the next day.

On Friday, Joan led approximately four hundred soldiers to the fort of Les Tourelles. As they approached the fort, they glimpsed the enemy and realized they were outnumbered two-to-one. The English, realizing their advantage, rushed out of the towers shouting and charging violently, but the easy victory they anticipated did not come to pass. The French fought bravely and effectively and forced the English into a defensive position.

Joan's leadership in battle amazed the experienced officers who fought alongside her. Alençon recalled, "In all her acts, aside from the facts of war, she was just a simple girl. But in war she was very expert, whether to carry a lance, to assemble an army, to order a battle, or to dispose the artillery. All marveled to see how in military matters she acted with as much sagacity and foresight as if she had been a captain, making war for twenty or thirty years. It was especially in the placing of artillery that she well understood herself."[116]

Joan was the first to place a scaling ladder on the fort bridge to advance on the enemy.[117] It was at this point that an English arrow pierced through a gap in her plate armor between her neck and shoulder. Her initial reaction was to try to ignore the arrow protruding from her body and continue to fight. But she soon realized she needed medical attention. Her squires carried her away from the center of battle. She cried out in pain and wept.[118] The arrow was removed from her body.

After hours of fighting, the French succeeded in forcing the English to retreat to the towers. By 8:00 p.m., Dunois thought it was time to withdraw the troops into the city. Joan asked him to wait and he obliged. Meanwhile, she rode to a vineyard nearby and prayed by herself. Dubois recalled what happened next: "Then she came back from that place, at once seized her standard in hand and placed herself on the parapet of the trench, and the moment she was there the English trembled and were terrified. And the King's soldiers regained courage and began to go up, charging against the boulevard without meeting the least resistance."[119]

Frightened, the English tried to retreat to the towers. The drawbridge collapsed and hundreds of English soldiers, who were weighed down by their armor, drowned in the Loire River. The remaining soldiers surrendered or left the city.

The next morning, Sunday, May 8, 1429, the English army appeared in full armor outside the walls of Orléans. Joan and her army stood in attention guarding the city. For an hour, the English and French stared each other down. Then the English turned around and walked away. In the words of Sacred Scripture revealing the fate of Saint Michael's enemies in battle, "there was no longer any place for them [there]" (Rv 12:8).

The cathedral bells tolled and the people rejoiced. Nine days after Joan's arrival, Orléans was free.

Coronation and Capture

With the liberation of Orléans behind her, Joan focused on her next task: the coronation of the rightful king of France. When she woke the next day, she did not participate in the celebrations in Orléans. Instead, she and her companions, including Dunois and other officers, set out to see King Charles, who was residing in Loches, ninety miles south of Orléans. For Charles to be accepted as the true king of France, it was important that he be crowned according to French tradition—in the city of Reims, which had become allied with the Burgundians. The immediate obstacle to the coronation was securing safe passage to Reims. The English controlled several towns that would make a journey to Reims dangerous. Joan intended to ask the king for men-at-arms to help her reclaim these towns for France. When Joan and her companions arrived in Loches, the king granted them an audience. Despite skepticism from his counselors, he agreed to supply them with an army.

Over the next few weeks, the French army reconquered the Loire Valley, Jargeau, Meung, Beaugency, and Patay. Alençon commanded the army and Joan provided key leadership, as she did in Orléans. Despite these important victories, the war was not over and many areas in France were not safe for French loyalists. The royal caravan left for Reims on June 29, 1429, under the protection of Joan, Alençon, Dunois, and thousands of knights and men-at-arms. When the king arrived in Reims on July 16, he was welcomed enthusiastically by most of the people, although some Burgundian loyalists left rather than celebrate the coronation of the French king; among them was Bishop Pierre Cauchon, who had helped negotiate the Treaty of Troyes and would play a central role in Joan's death.

The next day, the people watched and celebrated the coronation of their king. Charles took an oath to defend the people and the Church from all enemies. The archbishop of Reims anointed Charles on his chest, shoulders, elbows, and wrists in imitation of the anointing of King David and the other kings of Israel. Joan, her parents, her brothers, and Durand Laxart were among the distinguished guests. Joan wore full armor and carried her battle standard because, as she explained in her own words, "It had borne the burden, it had earned the honor."[120]

In the months following the coronation, Joan pressed the king to support military actions to end the war. It was not the act of war that appealed to her but the act of doing God's will. In August, she told Dunois, "I wish it were God's will for me to go away now and to lay down my armor and return to serving my parents by looking after the flocks with my sister and brothers, who would be so happy to have me at home."[121]

By this time, evil had taken root in the hearts of powerful men on both sides of the war who wished to punish Joan for her astonishing military prowess and success. Corrupted by jealousy, Georges de la Trémoïlle, a trusted royal counselor, tried to undermine the king's confidence in Joan by questioning her motives for future conquests. He wrote to Charles's wife and mother-in-law that there was "no doubt" that Joan intended to betray the king and control Paris herself.[122] Meanwhile, the Duke of Bedford, who had been winning the war until Joan inserted herself in his affairs, sought revenge on the pious maid. He leveraged his alliance with Philip of Burgundy by offering his envoys a financial reward for Joan's capture.[123]

King Charles listened to Joan's counsel urging swift and definitive military action, but he also listened to those around him who resented Joan's influence and were vying for power and influence themselves. Increasingly, Joan's advice conflicted with what he wanted to hear—which was that Philip of Burgundy would peacefully surrender Paris to him—and what his counselors obligingly told him. As a result, he consented to some of Joan's proposed military actions, but he did so slowly and without providing sufficient support. Once, the day after Joan was wounded in an attack, he abruptly interfered with the battle, ordering the army to stop fighting so he could pursue a peaceful resolution with Philip of Burgundy.

On May 24, 1430, Joan and her army of 350 soldiers took the Burgundian camp at Margny in the French loyalist city of Compiègne. But victory was fleeting. While the troops were occupied with battle, English reinforcements arrived and surrounded the town. Joan and her soldiers retreated to Compiègne, with the soldiers crossing the drawbridge to safety ahead of Joan, who always put herself in the most dangerous position. When the controllers of the gates saw the enemy approaching, they panicked, raising the drawbridge, closing the gates, and leaving Joan and only a few men outside. An enemy soldier grabbed Joan and handed her over to a lieutenant of Jean de Luxembourg, whose overlord was Philip of Burgundy.[124] Joan was now a prisoner in her own country, held captive by countrymen who were loyal to the enemy.

The King's Betrayal

In medieval warfare, it was a common practice for high-ranking prisoners to be held captive for some time and then be released upon the payment of a ransom by an ally. This was how Alençon earned his freedom after his capture at the Battle of Verneuil. But nothing was common about the French maid who was a master of the art of war. At eighteen years old, she was a hero to the French people and an embarrassment to the glory-seeking English and French leaders who failed where she succeeded. For jealous men on both sides of the war, the matter of Joan's debt would be settled not through the purchase of her freedom but through the purchase of her captivity; united in their vindictiveness and pride, they would conspire to punish and discredit the girl responsible for their humiliation.

On May 26, 1430, the day after news of Joan's capture reached Paris, the faculty of the University of Paris, represented by Bishop Cauchon, wrote to Philip of Burgundy asking for custody of Joan pursuant to their "duty of extirpating all errors against the faith and the scandal that follows such errors among simple Christian folk."[125] They implored, "We beseech you . . . that as soon as it can be done safely and conveniently, the aforesaid Joan be brought under our jurisdiction as a prisoner, since she is strongly suspected of various crimes smacking of heresy, so as to appear before us and a procurator of the Holy Inquisition."[126]

Bishop Cauchon had a strong connection to Philip, having served his father, John of Burgundy, who was murdered by the Armagnacs. A shrewd political maneuverer, Cauchon

had risen through the ranks of the Burgundian power struc-
ture through bold acts of loyalty to the English cause. In 1420,
he was promoted to bishop of Beauvais in the Burgundian
territory of Northern France; the same year, he negotiated
the Treaty of Troyes in England's favor. In 1422, he became
a counselor to King Henry VI of England, serving the Duke
of Bedford in his war efforts and living comfortably in Beauvais in anticipation of an English victory. Then, in a matter
of weeks in 1429, Joan shattered Cauchon's ambitions to
be a top-ranking churchman in English-controlled France.
Upon Charles's coronation in Reims, the people of Beauvais
pledged their loyalty to the French king, and Cauchon was
forced to flee to English-controlled Rouen.

On July 14, Cauchon hand-delivered a letter from the
University of Paris faculty to the Duke of Luxembourg. It
read: "The woman commonly called Joan the Maid, now
prisoner, must be sent to the King [of England] to be delivered over to the Church for trial, because she is suspected of
many crimes, sorceries, idolatry, intercourse with demons,
and other matters relative to faith and against faith."[127]

That same day, Cauchon went to see Philip of Burgundy.
On behalf of himself and the king of England, he offered
10,000 gold écus, the modern equivalent of 500,000 dol-
lars, to have Joan handed over to him to be tried for crimes
against the Church. Philip delivered news of Cauchon's offer
to his faithful ally, Luxembourg.

Meanwhile, Luxembourg received no communication
from King Charles, who owed his kingship and kingdom
to Joan. It was expected that the king would offer a ransom

for Joan's freedom or propose a prisoner swap—Joan for the English Earl of Suffolk—but he did neither.

Consistent with his allies' wishes, and because Cauchon's offer was the only offer on the table, Luxembourg sold Joan to the English for 10,000 gold écus. He received payment on December 6 and arranged for Joan's transfer.

On December 23, 1430, Joan arrived at her new cell in a castle occupied by the Earl of Warwick in Rouen. The cell was suffocatingly small: six and a half feet wide, with a window at one end, a toilet at the other, and a bed in between. Chains with iron bands adorned the walls and the foot of the bed; they would be used to restrain Joan day and night by her waist and wrists, with additional shackles placed on her ankles at night.[128]

Twice while in Luxembourg's custody, Joan had tried to escape, once jumping from a window and surviving a sixty-foot drop to the ground (which would have killed most people but only knocked Joan unconscious).[129] Bedford had purchased his prisoner with good money. He expected to be redeemed with a conviction and execution. His underlings were not about to let her get away.

A Trial Devoid of Justice

Joan's trial was a sham from the start. Cauchon had one objective: to convict Joan of a crime against the Church and turn her over to secular authorities to be burned at the stake. He left nothing to chance, seizing the role of judge and interrogator, enlisting the help of biased authorities, making threats against free-thinking participants, and, when all else failed, resorting to lies. Jean d'Estivet, the chief prosecutor, made no attempt to hide his hatred for Joan during the proceedings. Jean le Maître, the judge who served alongside Cauchon, harbored no ill will for Joan but was willing to sacrifice the innocent teenage girl to save himself. "I see clearly that if I do not proceed as the English desire, I am looking at my own imminent death," he said.[130]

The first stage of the trial lasted from January 9 to March 26, 1431. Beginning on February 21, Cauchon and Estivet interrogated Joan for five to seven hours a day in front of dozens of theologians, attorneys, and other experts and professionals who were being paid by England for their services.[131] Often, the interrogators misquoted her words and presented information in a confusing way, hoping to trick her into saying something that could be used to convict her. They failed.

At nineteen years old, Joan handled her interrogation like an experienced theologian and rhetorician—in other words, like the eighteen-year-old Saint Catherine of Alexandria, who, under extreme stress, debated and converted fifty philosophers with her wise words. Joan was treated inhumanely by agents of the one true Church. Every day for months, she was deprived of light, air, food, and clean water. In addition, she was forced to wear iron cuffs that tore at her skin, fight off attackers intending to violate her chastity, and undergo hours of hostile questioning, all while being denied the sacraments, for which she repeatedly asked. Throughout the process, Joan gave simple, theologically sound, and even brilliant answers to hundreds of questions presented to her in bad faith.

On the first day of her interrogation, Joan was asked to "swear on this book of the Holy Gospels to tell the whole

truth concerning everything that will be asked of you."¹³²
Holding the missal, she swore to tell the truth about matters
relating to the trial—including her actions in war, knowledge of the Faith, and even her upbringing—but not revelations given to her by God. "Even if you cut my head off,
I will not reveal anything, for God asks me to keep these
revelations secret," she added.¹³³

The matter of asking Joan to swear to tell the truth was
not merely procedural. It was part of the scheme to convict
her of heresy. Canon law prohibited excessive oath taking.
Thus, over the course of weeks of the trial, the interrogators
repeatedly asked her to swear to tell the truth, hoping to trick
her to help them build a case against her. She always refused,
answering that she had already given the oath asked of her.

Trick questions were a routine part of the interrogation
process, prompting some of Joan's most brilliant moments
of the trial. When asked, "Do you consider yourself in a state
of grace?" Joan refused to say "yes," and fall into the trap of
claiming to know what the Church teaches a person cannot
know with certainty, or "no," and fall into the trap of testi-
fying to having sinned against God. Instead, she said, "If I
am not in the state of grace, may God put me there—and if
I am, may He keep me there."¹³⁴ The notary, who recorded
the exchange, admitted that he was "much astonished" by
her perfect and holy answer.¹³⁵

Some trick questions were so dangerous that Joan refused
to answer them. For example, when she was asked, "Did
you go to Holy Communion at [feasts other] than Easter?"
Joan simply replied, "Go to the next question."¹³⁶ There was
no way for Joan to answer this question without giving the

enemy the opportunity to use her own words against her because Catholics must be in a state of grace to receive the Eucharist and they must confess mortal sins to be in a state of grace. If she answered yes, she would open the door to questions about whether she had gone to confession and why she needed absolution; any answer could be twisted to accuse her of sinfulness. If she answered no, she would be accused of lack of holiness.

Throughout the trial, Cauchon returned to the topic of Joan's wearing of men's clothing repeatedly. He intended to convict Joan of heresy by relying on a discredited interpretation of the prohibition in Deuteronomy 22:5 that "a woman shall not wear anything that pertains to a man." Theologians had clarified that the prohibition—like many others in the same chapter of the Old Testament book—could not be interpreted legalistically.[137] As Saint Thomas Aquinas had explained, it was acceptable for a woman to wear men's clothing and vice versa "on account of some necessity, either in order to hide oneself from enemies, or through lack of other clothes, or for some similar motive."[138]

Trial testimony should have acquitted Joan based on an honest interpretation of Sacred Scripture. Joan testified that she wore men's clothing for practical reasons in battle and for her own protection, before and during the trial. Guillaume Manchon, the principal court clerk at the trial, testified that Joan needed to wear men's clothing during the trial because "at night her guards tried to violate her . . . [and] it was only the tightly laced pants that discouraged her jailers."[139]

On Palm Sunday, Joan was told she could go to Mass if she wore a dress. In defense of her chastity, she declined.

During Holy Week, Estivet began the lengthy process of reading the seventy articles of indictment that had been prepared by Cauchon and his assessors and eliciting her response to each. The articles included the following outlandish accusations:

- Her mother was a witch and a sorcerer.
- She promised to kill the enemies of the Dauphin by magic.
- She said that God loves the king of France and hates the English.
- She was a vicious commander in war with a lust for blood.
- She worked only for her own material gain, for riches and honors.
- Her refusal to wear women's clothing is blasphemous, heretical, and a failure in submission to the will of the Church.[140]

On Holy Saturday, interrogations continued in her cell. When asked if she believed she was subject to the authority of the pope, cardinals, archbishops, bishops, and other prelates of the Church, she responded, "I am the servant of all—but Our Lord's first."[141]

By April 12, Cauchon and his team had condensed the seventy articles to twelve. He sent them to the University of Paris for consideration, but the faculty failed to reach a consensus about her guilt. Meanwhile, a group of priests in Rouen raised concerns with Cauchon about the lack of integrity and legality of the trial.

On April 16, Joan became violently ill after eating a piece of fish. Bedford feared she would die before Cauchon's team could have her burned at the stake, so he sent a doctor to care for her. Two days later, while she was still recovering, Cauchon and seven assessors went to her cell and threatened to torture her if she did not accept the findings of the Church against her. Joan told Cauchon that she was already in great danger of death. She asked him to hear her confession, give her Holy Communion, and bury her in consecrated ground. He responded that he would not give her the sacraments until she submitted to the Church's demands.

Two weeks later, her captors brought Joan to the dungeon, where a master executioner and nine judges awaited her arrival amid a dark room containing instruments of torture. Unwilling to confirm the lies the Church had presented to her, she exclaimed, "If you tore my limbs and threatened me so far as death, I would never say anything other than what I have already. And if I did so, I would later claim that you drew it out of me by force." The master executioner left the room without doing anything. The judges voted ten to three against torturing Joan.[142]

On May 19, Cauchon read the conclusion of the University of Paris aloud to the judges: forty-two of the forty-seven faculty members agreed that Joan was a heretic and must be handed over to the secular authorities for punishment unless she retracted her testimony and admitted the truth of the Church's accusations against her. When a cleric presented the conclusion to Joan, she boldly responded, "What I said and maintained at my trial, I still assert now. . . . And if I were to be condemned, and I saw the fire set, the wood prepared, and the executioner ready to throw me into the flames, even in the midst of the fire I would say nothing other than what I have previously said. And what I have sworn I will maintain even to my death."[143]

On May 24, in front of a large crowd at a cemetery of the church of Saint-Ouen, Joan's accusers presented her with a document and asked her to sign it. Joan was illiterate, which they knew. She asked that it be read aloud by a priest and said she would sign it if he advised her to. A priest, Joan Massieu, was by her side and he read the document to her. Chaos erupted. Guillaume Erart, a theologian and one of the judges, shouted at her, "You will sign right now! Otherwise fire will consume you before this day is over!" People in the crowd started throwing stones at her. The king's secretary placed a pen in her hand and she drew a circle on the paper with an *X* in it.[144]

The document she signed contained a statement of no more than eight lines; it contained a promise that she would not bear arms, wear men's clothing, or cut her hair. The document that was entered into the official trial record was much longer; it contained an admission that Joan was a "miserable sinner" guilty of many offenses, including lying, blaspheming, summoning evil spirits, killing out of a desire for the shedding of human blood, wearing a shameful and immodest dress against the decency of nature, and other sins against God and her fellow man. The official document also contained a promise that she would "never through exhortation or other means return to the aforesaid errors, for which it has pleased God to remove [her]."[145]

Joan's sentence—lifetime imprisonment—was read aloud. She was led back to her cell and was given a dress to wear. She put the dress on and submitted to having her head shaved as punishment.

Three days later, she asked her guards to remove her chains so she could use the toilet. When they did, they tore off her dress and refused to give it back, instead giving her the male clothing she had worn before. She wore the male clothing from then on. Cauchon visited her in her cell the next day to "catch" her relapse of sin. Two days later, he met with thirty-seven judges and assessors to inform them about her actions. Most of the men advised him to give her another chance before handing her over to secular authorities for punishment. But it was not the men's advice that Cauchon was after; it was their witness.

Burning at the Stake

On the morning of May 30, 1431, Joan woke up to a great blessing and a great terror. On that day, the eve of the feast of Corpus Christi, after being denied the sacraments for months, she would finally be permitted to confess and receive Jesus Christ, Body, Blood, Soul, and Divinity, in the Most Holy Eucharist. The intimacy with Jesus, obtained while in a state of grace, would give her the strength and courage to face the same cruel fate that had awaited Saint Margaret and Saint Catherine centuries before: she would die a painful death at the hands of eager executioners.

Fr. Martin Ladvenu administered the sacraments and then he and his fellow Dominican friar, Fr. Isambart de la Pierre, accompanied by more than eight hundred soldiers with axes and swords, led Joan to the Old Market Place of

Rouen near the church of Saint-Sauveur.[146] A large crowd had gathered. Joan's parents and neighbors from Domrémy were there, as were others who knew the accusations against her were lies perpetrated by the wounded egos of prideful men. Even before they caught a glimpse of the maid, they could see that preparations had been made for her execution; most harrowing was the pile of wood that sat at the foot of the stake.

Cauchon and his collaborators began the day's events by repeating the narrative they had crafted justifying their actions. Nicholas Midi, a theologian who played an active role in the trial, delivered a lengthy sermon declaring Joan to be an "incorrigible heretic who had relapsed into error and is unworthy of any pity."[147] Cauchon made the official announcement of Joan's guilt, proclaiming her "relapsed and heretic," and then he left. Joan turned to Father Ladvenue and Father Isambart and said, "With God's help, I shall be with Him in paradise."[148]

Instead of being sentenced by the secular judges, as was custom, the English executioner, Geoffrey Therage, seized Joan and took her to the stake.[149] Therage had a special hatred for the girl who had prevented the English domination of France, and so he performed his job with vigor.

Joan saw the torches that would ignite her body and deliver her soul to her Savior in heaven—and she collapsed, trembling and weeping in fear.[150] She knelt on the ground and asked the crowd to pray for her. She then asked God to forgive the men whose actions had brought her to this point. Someone placed a paper hat on her head that read, "Heretic—Relapsed—Apostate—Idolatress."[151]

Perhaps inspired by Saint Margaret, who achieved her legendary escape holding the symbol of Christ's sacrificial love, Joan asked for a cross. An English soldier was moved with pity and he made her a cross from two sticks on the wood pile and gave it to her. Gratefully, she kissed it and put it on her skin under her clothing, close to her heart. She then asked for a crucifix to gaze upon at her death. Father Isambart retrieved the processional cross from the church; when he returned with it, she kissed it and held it for a few seconds, and then he held it up high so she could fix her eyes on the image of the innocent, all-loving, crucified Christ.

Therage aggressively chained her hands behind her back around the stake. She prayed out loud as he lit the kindling and the fire started to rise and engulf the stake, with flames searing her skin and smoke choking her breath. Father Ladvenue and Father Isambart remained close to her throughout the horrible event. They recalled her final moment, "We heard her from the midst of the fire calling on her Saints and her Archangel. . . . Then, as her head fell forward, in a sign that she was fervent in the faith of God, she gave a great cry of 'JESUS!'"[152]

As her body burned, her soul escaped the sinfulness of the world of men, joining her loving Savior—the King of the Universe—and the angels and saints in heaven for eternity.

Meanwhile, Bedford ordered Therage to subdue the flames to reveal the dead body to the crowd. Therage complied and then he resumed his task of applying oil, sulfur, and charcoal to reduce the body to ash. This is when Therage, who only moments before had been consumed with hatred for the dead girl, realized with fear and regret that he had killed a holy disciple of Christ. Despite his best efforts and in defiance of the laws of nature, Joan's heart remained intact and full of blood. It would not burn. So close to the Sacred of Heart of Jesus was Joan's heart that it could not be consumed by the flames of this world.

France Would Remain French—and Catholic

The war continued for another twenty-two years after Joan's death. Under the leadership of King Charles, the French steadily drove the English out of their country, recapturing Paris in 1437 and Rouen in 1449. By 1453, the war was over. The French had taken back all their cities and England would never again try to bring France under English rule.

In Joan's time, France and England were both Catholic countries loyal to the one, holy, catholic, and apostolic Church. In the decades following the war, however, England would fall to the anti-Catholic influences of a new religious movement, Protestantism, that would swiftly stamp out Catholicism as the majority religion.

One hundred years after Joan's death, King Henry VIII of England would reject the authority of the Church over his personal and public affairs. Motivated by his desire to annul a valid marriage and marry his mistress, which is an impossibility in the one true Church that was founded by Jesus Christ, Henry would claim supremacy over the Catholic Church in England.[153] He would seize Church assets and appoint himself the head of the new established church, the Church of England. As the non-Catholic head of the English church, Henry would get his "annulment"—and three others. In all, Henry would have six wives, beheading two of them. Protestantism would take root in England and Catholics would become a persecuted minority. Most of the saints England would produce from then on would be martyrs who would die at the hands of English Protestants.

While France would suffer from many problems and would itself declare independence from the Catholic Church in 1905 (adopting a policy of separation of church and state), it would remain largely Catholic. Protestantism would not take hold in France as it would in England, either during or in the aftermath of the Reformation. For nearly six hundred years, Catholicism would continue to be the largest religion of the French people; it would remain a part of the cultural fabric of the country even as secularism spread throughout the country and the world. Significantly, in the years after the war, France would produce some of the Catholic Church's most beloved saints, including Saint Francis de Sales (1622), Saint Vincent de Paul (1660), Saint Margaret Mary Alacoque (1690), Saint Louis de Montfort (1716), Saint Jean-Baptiste de La Salle (1719), Saint John Vianney (1859), Saint Catherine Labouré (1876), Saint Bernadette of Lourdes (1879), Saint Thérèse of Lisieux, and Saint Elizabeth of the Trinity (1906).

All of these saints knew Joan's story. Saint Thérèse of Lisieux was especially influenced by the French teenager who courageously gave her life to do God's will.

A Heretic Becomes a Saint

Joan's family and friends were among the many people in France who knew that Joan had been wrongly convicted because they knew her to be a good and holy girl who sought nothing outside of God's will. It was Joan's mother and two of her brothers who asked the Holy See to open an investigation of Joan's trial. There had already been two local investigations launched—one by King Charles shortly after he entered Rouen in 1449 and another by cardinal legate Guillaume d'Estouteville two years later—that had revealed the biased and devious methods of Cauchon and his accomplices.

On June 11, 1455, Pope Calixtus III ordered an appeal of Joan's conviction. The trial took place over the course of several months and included the testimony of witnesses who knew Joan at different stages of her life, including those who were present at her trial. On July 7, 1456, at the bishop's residence in Rouen, the tribunal overturned Joan's conviction, declaring the trial illegal and unjust.

For centuries, Joan was honored as a hero in France as the Church sustained the embarrassment of having convicted as a heretic one of God's most loyal servants. In 1909, 478 years after Joan ascended to heaven to spend eternity with her Lord and King, Pope Pius X beatified Joan in the Notre Dame cathedral in Paris. On May 16, 1920, Pope Benedict XV canonized Joan, officially recognizing her as a saint of the Catholic Church.

A statement Joan made during her condemnation trial reveals the wisdom that made her a saint: "It is better to obey my sovereign Lord God rather than men."[154]

Saint José Luis Sánchez del Río

Saint José Luis Sánchez del Río was barely a teenager when he heroically gave his life for Christ. He loved his Catholic faith, his family, and his country. Mexico was a sacred place—the site of one of the most amazing miracles of all time. It is where, in the sixteenth century, Our Lady of Guadalupe appeared to Saint Juan Diego, leading to the conversion of nine million Mexicans in only nine years,[155] and millions more worldwide throughout the centuries. But in the early twentieth century, a Mexican dictator saw the Catholic Church as a threat to his power. He used violence to try to stamp out dissent and force the Mexican people to abandon their faith. José knew it was not God's plan for him to sit idly by as others fought for the right of the Mexican people to practice their faith.

Inspired by the love of Our Lady, as well as the courage of Saint Juan Diego and Blessed Anacleto González Flores, José voluntarily left the safety and security of his family to join the Cristeros, the rebel army fighting for Christ. At fourteen years old, José was considered too young to fight, so he had to ask special permission to join the Cristeros and assist them in other ways. He was accepted into a Cristeros camp, where the soldiers gave him the nickname "Tarcisius," after the twelve-year-old martyr who died protecting the Eucharist in the third century. The nickname was prophetic. Like Tarcisius, José would be chosen for a difficult mission; he would show tremendous fortitude and devotion and would die a child martyr. While he would lose his earthly life, he would gain eternal life with God in heaven—and his story would inspire people of all ages to be heroic witnesses to the truth that Christ is King.

A Catholic Childhood in a Catholic Country

José was born on March 28, 1913 in Sahuayo, Michoacán, Mexico,[156] during the Mexican Revolution, a time of significant political upheaval in the country and an awakening of Catholic social teaching throughout the universal Church. José's parents, Don Macario Sánchez and Maria del Río Arteaga, were Catholic, as were nearly all of their fellow countrymen. Macario and Maria raised their children in the Church. Together, they went to Mass, received the sacraments, and prayed the Rosary as a family. They had a strong devotion to Our Lady of Guadalupe.

SAINTLY INSPIRATION:
OUR LADY OF GUADALUPE AND SAINT JUAN DIEGO

Juan Diego Cuauhtlatoatzin was born in the Aztec Empire in Cuauhtitlan, Mexico in 1474.[157] He was an indigenous native of the Chichimecas tribe and was raised according to the pagan beliefs of the Aztecs.[158] The Aztecs believed there were many gods who ran the world, who would punish them—for example, by withholding rain or the rising of the sun—if they did not appease the gods' insatiable appetite for human blood. As a result, the Aztecs engaged in human sacrifice—and also cannibalism—on a scale exceeding any other civilization.[159]

The law of the Aztecs required one thousand human sacrifices every year in all towns with a temple, resulting in at least fifty thousand sacrificial killings a year and probably more.[160] The sacrifices were not considered shameful events. On the contrary, rites of "priests" ripping out the beating hearts of humans took center stage at huge feasts and festivals, accompanied by music, dancing, and merriment. Victims were often of considerable status and nearly always from friendly city-states that shared the Aztec culture. They were not pitied, but honored.[161] As a result, victims generally did not resist their slaughter, and when they did, it was considered a bad omen.[162] Rather, they sang and danced to their deaths "with great joy and gladness."[163] One group of victims that did resist, however, were children.[164] The Aztecs who led children to their deaths encouraged tears—even tearing their finger nails off to produce tears—because they believed one of the gods would only accept the sacrifice of a child if the child cried.[165] All child victims were locals of noble lineage, offered by their own parents.[166]

The Aztec empire lasted from 1428 to August 13, 1521, when Hernan Cortes and three hundred Spanish soldiers conquered Mexico for Spain with the capture of the emperor, Cuauhtemoc.[167] Three years later, twelve Franciscan friars, known as "the twelve apostles," arrived to bring Christianity to the New World. They were followed by the Dominicans in 1526 and the Augustinians in 1533.[168] The missionaries had their work cut out for them. They preached the Gospel, revealing the existence of the one true God, the source of all love and goodness, who condemns idolatry, human sacrifice, and the unjust treatment of any of His children. But the Aztec temples were a constant reminder of the false gods the indigenous people had worshipped for generations, and so the people clung to their pagan beliefs. The missionaries were intent on liberating the people from the evil influence of their idols. In 1525, they began destroying the temples—an action that, according to Friar Juan de Zumarraga, made the natives "sad and hurt."[169]

Friar Zumarraga arrived in Mexico in 1529 and was appointed bishop in 1530. On August 27, 1529, he wrote a letter to the king of Spain explaining the challenges of evangelization in the New World. A major obstacle for the missionaries was the sinful actions of Spaniards who claimed to be Christians and yet treated the natives cruelly.[170] Friar Zumarraga's letter complained of Spaniards doing "many dishonest and unlawful things" to the native people. His words conveyed a sense of desperation. "If God does not provide a remedy from His hand," he wrote, "this land is about to be lost."[171]

Despite immense challenges, the missionaries baptized thousands of native people, who appreciated the kindness of the Christians and recognized the truth of the Faith "written on [their] hearts" (2 Cor 3:2).

Juan Diego was among them. He had only been a Christian for a few weeks when the Mother of God chose him for a special mission that would, as Pope John XXIII said, demonstrate "Her calling as a Mother" and "symbolize a kiss of two races," united in Christ.[172]

On December 9, 1531, only a few weeks after his baptism, Juan Diego heard the harmonious and sweet song of a choir of birds as he walked to Mass on a Saturday morning.[173] He found himself at the foot of Tepeyac Hill. He looked up and saw a shiny white cloud and a rainbow: the sign of the everlasting covenant between God and all mortal beings (see Gn 9:11–17). He was amazed and said to himself, "Am I by luck worthy of what I see? . . . Perhaps I am there where our old ancestors, our grandparents have said: in the land of the flowers, in the land of corn, of our flesh, of our sustenance, perhaps in the land of Heaven."[174]

The birds stopped singing and he heard the delicate voice of a woman calling his name: "Juanito, Juan Dieguito." He climbed the hill and found himself standing before a Maiden who radiated with heavenly beauty. She was a young, native, pregnant mother, "clothed in sun" with "the moon at her feet," as described in Revelation 12:1.

Juan Diego prostrated himself before her and she spoke. She told him who she was—"the perfect always, Virgin, Holy Mary, Mother of the true God"—and what she desired—to have a church built on Tepeyac Hill for the purpose of bringing God to the Mexican people and the world. She explained, "I will give Him to all the people in my personal love, in my compassionate sight, in my help, in my salvation; because I am truly your compassionate mother, yours and those men in this land who are one, and the rest of the various nations of men."[175]

Our Lady told Juan Diego to go to the bishop of Mexico and tell him to build her a church. "Tell him everything, all that you have seen and admired, and what you have heard," she said.[176] He obeyed and walked straight to the house of Bishop Zumarraga in the city of Mexico.

When Juan Diego arrived at the house, the servants treated him distrustfully and made him wait a long time before informing the bishop of his presence. The bishop immediately agreed to see Juan Diego, but when he heard this simple man's fantastic story, he did not believe him.

Juan Diego returned to Tepeyac Hill and pleaded with the Blessed Mother to entrust Her important mission to someone the bishop would believe—a noble person, someone who was well known, respected, and honored. Our Lady responded that many people serve her—but this mission was his, not theirs. She said, "It is necessary that *you, personally*, go, beg, that *through your intercession* my wish, my will, be accomplished."

She told Juan Diego to go to the bishop again. He obeyed. Again, the servants made him wait a long time. Again, Bishop Zumarraga listened—and again, he did not believe. On this visit, the bishop asked Juan Diego to bring him a sign that would prove his story. When Juan Diego left, he headed for Tepeyac Hill and the bishop told two servants to follow him. The servants began following Juan Diego, but they lost him. Instead of admitting failure, they told the bishop that they discovered Juan Diego to be a deceiver, liar, and sorcerer.

When Juan Diego arrived at Tepeyac Hill, the Blessed Mother was waiting for him. She ordered him to return the following day to receive the sign for the bishop. But the following day, December 12, brought great distress. He discovered that his uncle, Juan Bernardino, was very ill and was expected to die. Juan Diego loved his uncle like a father. So when Juan Bernardina begged Juan Diego to go to the convent of Santiago Tlaltelolco to ask a priest to confess him and prepare him for death, he consented. Juan Diego set out to walk to the convent. He took a different route so he would not pass Tepeyac Hill. Our Lady was waiting for him on the new path. Surprised and embarrassed, Juan Diego told her what had happened. He promised to come back the following day, after he found a priest for his dying uncle. She consoled him and said, "Do not fear of that disease nor any other disease, nor any piercing, afflictive thing. Am I, who am your mother, not here? Are you not under my shadow, and my shelter? Am I not the fountain of your joy?"[177]

She told him his uncle had been healed. He believed her and implored her to send him to the bishop with a sign. She told him to go to the top of the hill, cut the flowers there, and bring them down the hill to her. He obeyed, even though he knew there were no flowers on the rocky hill—especially not in December when there was ice on the ground. When Juan Diego walked up the hill, he found a beautiful garden of vibrant, fresh flowers with a soft scent. He gathered them in his tilma, a cloak made of cactus fiber, and brought them to her. She took the flowers in her hands and placed them back in his tilma.

Juan Diego returned to the bishop's house for the third time. Again, he was made to wait a very long time. But this time, when he was led into the room to see Bishop Zumarraga, he did not meet the disbelieving eyes of a skeptical cleric—because, once Juan Diego entered, he extended his tilma, releasing a panoply of fragrant flowers to the floor, and exposing an image of the Blessed Mother on his tilma. The image of Our Lady appeared as Juan Diego had seen her, and as it is miraculously preserved today.

Together, Bishop Zumarraga and Juan Diego went to Tepeyac Hill so Juan Diego could show the bishop where Our Lady wanted her church to be built. Then, accompanied by the bishop's family, Juan Diego went to see his uncle and found him in perfect health. Juan Bernardino told Juan Diego that Our Lady had appeared to him and healed him; he described her exactly as she appeared to Juan Diego in person and to the bishop on the tilma.

Bishop Zumarraga obeyed Mother Mary and built her church. Devotion to Our Lady of Guadalupe spread quickly, freeing the native people from a false religion that had blinded them to the most basic truths of the human experience, including the sanctity of human life. Within nine years, Our Lady of Guadalupe converted nine million natives to Catholicism—nearly two thousand a day.[178] Within twenty-five years, she converted virtually all of Mexico.[179]

From Spanish Rule to Independence to the Outlawing of Catholicism

Our Lady of Guadalupe promised to be a "compassionate mother" to the people of Mexico, but she never promised to make their country a heaven on earth. No country governed by men can be free of the stain of sin and the suffering of this world.

For three hundred years, from 1521 to 1821, Spain governed Mexico as a Spanish colony, called New Spain.[180] Because of its Christian missionary and evangelization efforts in the New World, Spain had been granted a special patronage by the Vatican, called *Patronato Real*, to act on behalf of the Catholic Church.[181] Much good came of this relationship. The Catholic Church was a major landowner in New Spain and used its resources to tend to the spiritual and physical needs of the Mexican people. In addition to offering the sacraments, the Church operated hospitals, schools, and orphanages[182] and fueled economic growth by providing loans at low interest rates. But there were abuses too. Not all priests were holy men, but all were "above the law." A body of laws, called the *fueros*, exempted Catholic clergy from standing trial for engaging in illegal activities. By making the Church the protector of wrongdoing, the *fueros* damaged the Church's moral authority and created resentment all around.

By the eighteenth century, many government officials became envious of the Church's cultural influence and substantial infrastructure in New Spain. In 1767, the crown expelled all Jesuits from the colony and confiscated all their properties, including churches, universities, and seminaries.[183] It was a prelude to attacks on the Church on a much larger scale.

Mexico won its independence from Spain in 1821. Because of Spain's mistreatment of the Catholic Church, the movement for independence was at first deeply religious. But soon after Mexico became independent, a faction of Mexican intellectuals animated by the anti-Catholic French

Revolution rose to power. Benito Juarez, a skilled political maneuverer, became the leader of this movement, first as head justice of the Supreme Court (succeeding in ratifying anti-Catholic amendments to the constitution in 1857) and then as president of Mexico for fourteen years. Using the same tactics of the radicals of the French Revolution, he seized Church property and made Catholic clergy the employees of the state. He also barred government officials from attending Mass in an official capacity and restricted religious processions in the street.[184]

Juarez used force to further his agenda, but he also used argument and emotion. By tapping into a deep desire of the Mexican people to be governed as an independent state free of foreign interference—and by denigrating the Catholic Church as a foreign interest—he made supremacy of civil power over the Church a key tenet of Mexican nationalism. When he died in office in 1872, he was considered a national hero—and remained so throughout the nineteenth century and into the twentieth century.[185]

The most significant leader to succeed Juarez in the nineteenth century was Porfirio Diaz, who became president in 1884. Diaz was head of the anti-Catholic Freemasons in Mexico, but he was a pragmatist, not an ideologue. For twenty-seven years, he generally left the Church alone even as he ruled as a dictator. He did not go out of his way to help Catholics—for example, he refused to reinstate a formal relationship between Mexico and the Vatican or revoke the anti-Catholic provisions of the 1857 constitution—but he generally allowed them to practice their faith freely. Catholics welcomed the relative peace and stability, but they suffered in other ways. In contrast to political leaders and the few large landowners in Mexico who lived well, life was hard for most ordinary people. Poverty and malnutrition were rampant. Many Mexicans toiled in poor conditions, from dawn to dusk, six or seven days a week, earning grossly inadequate wages. The average life expectancy was thirty. Conditions were ripe for a revolution.[186]

The Mexican Revolution began in 1910 when Diaz sparked an armed rebellion by jailing a political opponent named Francisco I. Madero. Madero was a wealthy landowner who would be elected president in 1911 and then murdered in a coup in 1913. From 1910 to 1920, the Mexican people endured a civil war of armed regional conflicts, military coups, and political instability. The war became a training ground for radical revolutionary leaders intent on escalating Juarez's anti-Catholic policies. They included Francisco José Mugica, who called Catholic clergy "the most dismal, the most perverse enemy of the fatherland"; Victoriano Huerta, who justified the plundering of Church possessions to pay his army, saying, "Mexico can do without her priests, but cannot do without her soldiers"; and Plutarco Calles, a Freemason, who once declared publicly, "I have a personal hatred for Christ."[187]

The revolutionaries convened a constitutional convention in 1917, which resulted in the first socialist constitution in the history of the world.[188] Mugica wrote major portions of the document. The new law:

- outlawed Catholic schools;
- forbade the Catholic Church from holding, acquiring, or administering property for the

purpose of operating a church, seminary, convent, residence, school, hospital, or orphanage and transferred existing ownership to the state;

- forbade priests from voting, holding public office, commenting on political issues, wearing religious vestments in public, and inheriting property;
- banned public worship outside church buildings and banished all foreign-born priests from the country; and
- gave state legislatures the power to decide how many priests were allowed in each state.[189]

At first, most governors and legislators did not enforce the new constitution. This meant Catholics in most areas of the country continued to practice their faith as they did before. But the constitution made discrimination against Catholics the law of the land. It codified the deeply held belief of the revolutionaries seeking complete control of the culture and the economy, that the Church was a competitor for the people's loyalty and must be eliminated.

In 1924, Plutarco Calles became president. That same year, Mexico formalized relations with the Soviet Union, making Mexico the first country in the American continent to recognize the Soviet Union.[190]

Calles was intent on destroying the Mexican Catholic Church and stripping the people of their faith. One of his very first actions as president was to create a nationalized school system to form children supportive of his agenda. He, of course, was vehemently opposed to the Catholic Church's teaching that parents are the primary educators of their children. He once said, "We must now enter and take possession of the consciences of the children, of the consciences of the young, because they do belong and should belong to the Revolution. . . . I refer to education, I refer to the school . . . because the children and youth belong to the community; they belong to the collectivity, and it is the Revolution that has the inescapable duty to take possession of consciences, to drive out prejudices and to form a new soul of the nation."[191]

In 1926, he enforced a series of measures known as the Calles Laws that ordered civil and military authorities to offer public allegiance to Calles and fully implement the 1917 constitution. Accordingly, government troops took over churches—vandalizing them and instituting lay administrators—and closed all Catholic schools, putting all education under direct state control.

They closed Catholic orphanages and hospitals, removed crucifixes and religious images from buildings and homes, fined people for uttering the word "God," and fired on religious processions in the streets. When local citizens tried to defend their churches from attack, authorities resorted to bloodshed, executing parishioners to assume control of God's sacred spaces.[192]

Archbishop of Mexico José Mora y del Rio refused to comply with Calles's demands. Rather than allow the Church to be controlled and manipulated by one of her greatest enemies, on July 25, 1926, he ended all public religious services.[193] Until religious freedom returned to Mexico, the people would be forced to live without the sacraments.

Growing up in Calles's Mexico

José received the sacraments of Christian initiation amid the violence of the Mexican revolution and increasing hostility towards Catholics. He was baptized on April 3, 1913, in the Church of Saint James the Apostle in Sahuayo.[194]

That year, revolutionary generals took over the Mexican government and murdered President Madero, installing General Huerta as president for one year, until he was forced into exile and replaced by General Venustiano Carranza in 1915. José was confirmed in 1917, the year the new social-ist, anti-Catholic constitution became law. In 1920, Álvaro Obregón, Calles, and other revolutionary generals rebelled against President Carranza, who fled to Mexico City and was killed. Obregón was elected president in 1920. The following year, on the morning of November 14, 1921, Luciano Perez Carpio, an underling of the Obregón government, planted a bomb at the foot of the image of Our Lady of Guadalupe at the Basilica in Mexico City; the explosion destroyed every-thing in its vicinity, except the tilma, which was unharmed.[195]

In 1922, José received his First Holy Communion at the Church of Saint James the Apostle.[196] His godfather and sponsor was Rafael Picazo Sánchez, the mayor of Sahuayo.

José was a deeply religious child who was maturing into a faithful and virtuous young man. He went to Mass and confession frequently and prayed the Rosary daily. He con-sidered Jesus to be his best friend and he spoke and prayed to Him throughout every day.

José was eleven years old when Calles assumed power. Calles's dictatorship made José an outlaw, but it did not weaken his faith or abate his desire to do God's will. Father Fidel González, a postulator for the cause of José's canonization, remembered José as a "normal, healthy kid with a joyful character," who sought out God's intimate participation in His life through the sacraments, despite the danger it posed to his earthly life. He testified, "Though it put his life at risk since public worship was prohibited, he received the sacraments when he could. He prayed the holy rosary each day with his family. Despite being very young, José understood very well what Mexico was going through with the persecution."[197]

One of the most pernicious aspects of Calles's rule was the outlawing of religious instruction to children. Having been fully initiated into the Church—having becoming "enriched with a special strength of the Holy Spirit," "more perfectly bound to the Church," and "more strictly obliged to spread and defend the Faith by word and deed"[198]—José took it upon himself to teach the Faith to the younger children in his town, in obedience to Jesus's command: "Let the children come to me, and do not hinder them; for to such belongs the kingdom of heaven" (Mt 19:14).

Undaunted by the illegality of his obedience to God, José talked to the children about Jesus and took them to visit Him in the Blessed Sacrament. José's kindness, sincerity, and resourcefulness made him a natural leader and an effective teacher. Two of the children that José taught went on to become priests and found religious orders.[199]

The Catholic Church is the Mystical Body of Christ. It is physical and spiritual, human and divine, uniting all members intimately to Christ and each other. In Calles's Mexico,

José and his fellow countrymen did not suffer alone, because no member of the Church suffers alone. As the Church teaches: "If one member suffers anything, all the members suffer with him, and if one member is honored, all the members together rejoice."[200]

On November 18, 1926, Pope Pius XI expressed his solidarity with the suffering people of Mexico. He published an encyclical, *Iniquis Afflictisque* ("Unjust and Afflicted"), condemning "the enemies of the Common Father of all" and asking the universal Church to pray and implore Our Lady of Guadalupe "to ask of God that peace and concord may return to her people." Emphasizing the extreme and unprecedented nature of the attacks on the Mexican Church, he wrote:

> If in the first centuries of our era and at other periods in history Christians were treated in a more barbarous fashion than now, certainly in no place or at no time has it happened before that a small group of men has so outraged the rights of God and of the Church as they are now doing in Mexico, and this without the slightest regard for the past glories of their country, with no feelings of pity for their fellow-citizens. They have also done away with the liberties of the majority and in such a clever way that they have been able to clothe their lawless actions with the semblance of legality.[201]

Within two months, the first loose-knit armies of farmers began to form in Jalisco, Zacatecas, Guanajuato, and Michoacan (where José's family lived) to fight for "the rights of God and of the Church."²⁰² Known as the Cristeros for their battle cries, "Viva Cristo Rey!" and "Viva la Virgen de Guadalupe!" the soldiers sang hymns as they marched and prayed the Rosary at night. They were unskilled and poorly equipped at first, but they gained experience in battle and accumulated weapons, ammunition, and supplies from a loyal network of supporters throughout the country that included women and children.

The deeply religious Sánchez family was horrified by the government's persecution of God in the land blessed by the personal love of Our Lady of Guadalupe. They supported the Cristeros and their righteous cause. José's mother and aunt, Magdalena, smuggled food and supplies to the army. José's older brothers, Miguel and Guillermo, joined the army to fight.

Many battles between the Cristeros and the Federales, the federal army, occurred in Michoacan. The Federales were brutal in their treatment of soldiers and supporters. They frequently executed soldiers in public and also murdered priests, lay men and women, and even children. Bodies hanging from trees in the village square became a hallmark of Calles's Mexico and his war with the "one, holy, catholic and apostolic Church."²⁰³

A few months into the fighting, José traveled approximately sixty miles to Guadalajara to visit the grave of a hero and martyr of the Cristero War: Anacleto González Flores.

Saintly Inspiration:
Blessed Anacleto González Flores

Anacleto González Flores was born on July 13, 1888, in Tep-
atitlán, Jalisco, Mexico. He was the second of twelve children born to Catholic parents, Valentín González Sanitiz
and Maria Flores Navaho.[204] Similar to many Mexicans in
the nineteenth century, the González family suffered from
devasting poverty. They lived and worked in a tiny one-
room house. Together, they ate, slept, and made women's
shawls that they sold to nearby ranches to make ends meet.
A neighbor said the family was always struggling. For two
years while the children were young, Maria managed the
family and business while Valentín served a prison sentence
for protesting Porfirio Diaz's dictatorship.[205]

Anacelto was a curious and vivacious child. He was a
voracious reader who also loved music and dancing. He
had a special gift for organizing activities, which caused a
family friend—a priest—to give him the nickname "Maestro."[206] His parents could not afford to send him to Catholic school, so he attended the local government school which
was unapologetically anti-Catholic. Perhaps because of his
schooling, Anacleto was not particularly interested in religion when he was young. That changed when a missionary
visited his parish when he was seventeen years old. Anacleto
participated in a retreat led by the missionary and the experience unleashed in him a sense of wonder about the world
around him. He developed a more sophisticated interior life
and started reading books about philosophy, social morality,
and ethics.[207]

The priest who gave Anacleto his nickname noticed the Maestro was becoming a fine young man. He thought he would make a good priest, so he recommended him to the local high school seminary in San Juan de los Lagos.

Seminary was a time of deep reflection for Anacleto. He immersed himself in his studies in high school and then went on to attend the seminary in Guadalajara. During these formative years, Anacleto became a scholar and an activist with a deep love for the Eucharist and a passion for helping his fellow man. Pope Leo XIII's *Rerum Novarum* ("On Capital and Labor") had a profound influence on his thinking.

Published in 1891, *Rerum Novarum* was the Catholic response to social, political, and economic changes sweeping the developed world in the aftermath of the revolutions of 1848. Pope Leo XIII was concerned that the solution being embraced by a growing number of elites and laborers—the dehumanizing ideology of socialism—would spread and create greater distance between God's law and His people. Through *Rerum Novarum,* he made it clear that the pursuit of financial and societal goals must always be pursued in harmony with God's law. He wrote that the "power to rule comes from God" and should be exercised with a "fatherly solicitude" that considers the good of individuals and families; that the family has rights "prior" to those of the community and it is a "great and pernicious error" for the government to intrude into and exercise intimate control over the family; that government has a "duty of safeguarding private property by legal enactment and protection" because the right of private property belongs "naturally to individual persons" and to "a man in his capacity of head of a family"; that it is improper for socialists to exploit "the poor man's envy of the rich" to generate support for the unjust taking of private property; and that employers must respect the God-given dignity of employees with respect to wages and conditions because it is "neither just nor human so to grind men down with excessive labor as to stupefy their minds and wear out their bodies."

Rerum Novarum cultivated in Anacleto a strong sense of justice that filled his soul with courage, love, and a desire to act. He volunteered with the National Catholic Party—a political party that achieved remarkable success in its brief existence of two years, electing twenty-nine federal deputies, senators, and governors in four states[208]—while on vacation from seminary.

In July 1913, after four years at seminary, Anacleto discerned that his vocation was to live his faith in the world as a lay person, not through the priesthood. He took his calling seriously. He enrolled in law school, supporting himself by taking odd jobs, and anchoring all activities in the Faith. He joined and became a leader of the ACJM (Asociacion Catolica de la Juventud Mexicana), a lay organization founded by a Jesuit priest that activated young people to infuse Catholic values into all levels of public life in Mexico.[209] He helped found a Catholic newspaper, called *The Gladium*. He taught catechism to children and organized study groups with peers to discuss *Rerum Novarum* and other topics relevant to the plight of the Mexican people. There were many demands on the Maestro's time—but none was more important than worshipping God, the source of all truth and goodness. No matter how busy Anacelto was, he never missed daily Mass.

Someone once asked him what he enjoyed doing most. He replied, "Receiving Communion! The day I don't receive Communion, I am nothing; my life and equilibrium are missing."[210]

Anacleto was still in law school in 1917 when the new Constitution outlawing the free and open practice of Catholicism became the law of the land. At first, most governors ignored the new provisions. But in Jalisco, where Anacelto lived, legislators wasted no time seizing authority over Church affairs. They passed a law reducing the number of priests in Jalisco to one for every five thousand people and creating a multi-step application process for priests seeking a license to lawfully celebrate Mass and administer the sacraments. The law threatened priests with imprisonment and heavy fines for the "crime" of carrying out priestly duties without approval by the state.

Anacelto was deeply upset by the unholy overreach of the government. But his education and leadership experience had prepared him for this moment. With the help of friends, mostly through the ACJM, he organized a statewide boycott that crippled the state's economy and social life. Under his direction, Catholics avoided the purchase of all items except the bare necessities. They kept their children home from school. They attended peaceful demonstrations in the gallery of the legislature and on the streets, leading to the willing arrest of hundreds of Mexicans who sang and prayed joyfully in prison. After eight months, the government rescinded the law completely.

The victory in Jalisco was satisfying, but short-lived. Harassment and mistreatment of Catholics continued in Jalisco and throughout many Mexican states. In 1922, Anacleto earned his law degree, married Concha Guerrero Figueroa, and founded a new organization, called the Popular Union. The purpose of the Popular Union was to unite Mexicans in the defense of their God-given rights, especially the right to practice their Catholic faith. Membership quickly grew to more than 100,000. The following year, Anacleto became a leader of another new organization, the National League for the Defense of Religious Liberty, which was also created to unite Catholics in their opposition to religious persecution. The organizations merged in 1926.

In 1927, when the Cristeros took up arms to defend God, His Church, and the people of Mexico who were being denied the right to live as Catholics, Anacelto did not become a soldier, but he fought in another crucial way. Anacleto had been thinking about and practicing his faith—through his studies, political activity, and intimacy with God, always-present in the sacraments—for decades. He knew why the Cristeros were fighting and why it was important for the Mexican people to join their cause, and so, using his resourcefulness as the Maestro, he wrote and spoke directly to the Mexican people to earn their support. He wrote pamphlets and flyers, raised money for supplies, and delivered dynamic speeches stirring the hearts of his countrymen. He made it clear that obedience to God is the only path to salvation: "The country is a jail for the Catholic Church! We are not worried about defending our material interests because they come and go; but our spiritual interests, these we must defend because they are necessary to obtain our salvation."[211]

He asked the people to join the Cristeros, even unto death, but never in vain: "I know only too well that what is beginning now for us is Calvary. We must be ready to take up arms and carry our crosses. . . . If one should ask me what sacrifice I am asking of you in order to seal the pact we are going to celebrate, I will tell you in two words: your blood."[212]

Anacleto's courageous and effective advocacy made him a threat to Calles's crusade against the Church. Accordingly, government agents placed him high on their "watch list." On April 1, 1927, the infamously cruel General Jesus Maria Ferreira, chief of the Military Zone of Jalisco, arrested him, along with friends, at the home of the Vargas González family.

Ferreira and the torturers were brutal to Analceto: they hung him by his thumbs, beat and stabbed him, and cut the soles of his feet open, inflicting horrendous pain. They demanded he reveal the location of Archbishop Orozco y Jimenez of Guadalajara, who continued to celebrate the sacraments, including the ordination of young priests, but he refused, answering simply, "I know nothing! Long live Christ the King!"[213]

Anacleto asked his torturers to kill him last so he could comfort his friends in their final moments. After the murder of his friends, he turned to General Ferreira and said, "I die, but God does not die!"[214] He then told General Ferreira, "Soon you will present yourself before God. I will be your greatest intercessor."[215]

The torturers pierced Anacaleto on both sides of his back with a bayonette, perforating his lungs and causing him to collapse. They shot him at close range.

As he lay dying, Anacleto said one last time, "Viva Cristo Rey!"[216]

Pope Benedict XVI beatified Anacleto, along with eight other martyrs of the Mexican persecution, on November 20, 2005.[217]

A Young and Faithful Cristero

By the summer of 1927, not long after he visited Anacleto González Flores's grave, José made the decision to enlist in the Cristero army. He was only fourteen years old, so he asked his parents for permission. Initially, they resisted. But then he pleaded, "Mama, do not let me lose the opportunity to gain Heaven so easily so soon."[218] José's parents knew their son's pure heart and sincere faith. They agreed to let him go. Before departing, he proclaimed, "For Jesus Christ, I will do everything."[219]

José was smart and resourceful, but at fourteen years old, he was still a boy. He knew the Cristeros might not accept his help. He first tried to join the Cristeros at the Sahuayo camp, but the general turned him away for being too young. Undaunted, he and his friend, Trinidad Flores, set off to the Cristero camp in Cotija, approximately forty miles away. There, the Cristero commander, Prudencio Mendoza, asked, "What contribution can so small a boy make to our army?" José responded, "I ride well. I know how to tend horses, clean weapons and spurs, and how to fry beans and tortillas."[220]

General Mendoza initially refused the boys' enlistment. Impressed by José's determination, however, he relented and allowed them to stay, but not to fight as soldiers. He made José the aid of General Ruben Guizar Morfin.[221]

José lived, worked, and worshipped alongside the soldiers at camp. He performed simple, but critical, tasks to support the soldiers as they trained and prepared for battle. He carried water, prepared the fire, served food and coffee, washed dishes, fed the horses, and cleaned rifles.[222] Every day, he attended Mass with the soldiers. Every evening, he prayed the Rosary with them. His friendly and sincere nature quickly earned him the fondness of the older men who noticed and admired his deep faith.

Worshipping Jesus came as naturally to José as breathing. Even in front of the older men he admired, he was not embarrassed to display his piety at camp. He knelt before and received the Most Blessed Sacrament so reverently, the soldiers affectionately gave him the nickname "Tarcisius," after the early Christian martyr who also passionately loved and honored Christ in the Eucharist.

SAINTLY INSPIRATION: SAINT TARCISIUS

Beginning with the rule of Nero in AD 64 and ending with Constantine's Edict of Milan in AD 313, the early Christians endured brutal persecution in the Roman Empire. In the third century, Emperor Valerian terrorized Christians of all classes and rank. He ordered the immediate execution of Christian leaders, including all bishops, priests, and deacons, making martyrs of Pope Sixtus II, Cyprian of Carthage, and Saint Lawrence in the year 258. He confiscated the property of Christian men of senatorial and equestrian rank and ordered the execution of those who refused to apostatize. He also ordered the exile and confiscation of property of women who refused to apostatize.

Tarcisius was a twelve-year-old boy during Valerian's persecution of Christians.[223] He frequently went to the Catacombs of Saint Calixtus to gather with other Christians and participate in Holy Mass. He had a great love for the Eucharist and was probably an acolyte who assisted priests in the celebration of Mass. One day, when a priest asked for a volunteer to take the Eucharist to prisoners and the sick, Tarcisius volunteered. "Send me!" he exclaimed. "My youth will be the best shield for the Eucharist." The priest agreed and gave him the consecrated Hosts, saying to him, "Tarcisius, remember that a heavenly treasure has been entrusted to your weak hands. Avoid crowded streets and do not forget that holy things must never be thrown to dogs nor pearls to pigs. Will you guard the Sacred Mysteries faithfully and safely?"[224]

Tarcisius assured the priest that he would protect the Eucharist. "I would die rather than let go of them," he said.[225] He set out to minister to his fellow Christians, and on his way, some friends noticed him and asked him to join them. He refused and they noticed he was holding something close to his breast. They became suspicious and tried to pry it away from him, but he would not let go. They realized Tarcisius was a Christian and became fiercer in their attacks. They kicked him and threw stones at him. Still, Tarcisius clung tightly to the body and blood of Christ. A Praetorian Guard named Quadratus, who had secretly become a Christian, found him lying on the ground. Quadratus carried the boy to the priest. By the time they arrived, Tarcisius was already dead. He was still clutching the small linen bag containing the Eucharist.

An oral tradition of Roman martyrology holds that the Most Blessed Sacrament was not found on Tarcisius's body because, as Pope Benedict XVI explained, "The consecrated Host which the little Martyr had defended with his life, had become flesh of his flesh thereby forming, together with his body, a single immaculate Host offered to God."[226]

Tarcisius's body was immediately buried in the Catacombs of Saint Calixtus. His story became a source of strength for Christians living under Roman persecution—and remains an inspiration for Christians seeking to remain faithful to God in all areas of their lives today.

Pope Benedict XVI told Tarcisius's story to a general audience at Saint Peter's Square on August 4, 2010:

> St. Tarcisius' testimony and this beautiful tradition teach us the deep love and great veneration that we must have for the Eucharist: it is a precious good, a treasure of incomparable value; it is the Bread of life, it is Jesus himself who becomes our nourishment, support and strength on our daily journey and on the open road that leads to eternal life; the Eucharist is the greatest gift that Jesus bequeathed to us. . . .
>
> Dear friends! You lend Jesus your hands, your thoughts, your time. He will not fail to reward you,

giving you true joy and enabling you to feel where the fullest happiness is. St. Tarcisius has shown us that love can even bring us to give our life for an authentic good, for the true good, for the Lord.[227]

Heroic Love for Christ the King

General Morfin was impressed with José's diligence and commitment to the Cristero cause. He promoted his young aid to standard-bearer, making José responsible for riding next to him in combat, carrying the Cristero flag, and playing the bugle to communicate his orders to the troops.[228] The Cristero flag resembled the Mexican flag but contained two key additions: the image of Our Lady of Guadalupe and the words "Viva Cristo Rey y Nuestra Senora de Guadalupe" (Long Live Christ the King and Our Lady of Guadalupe).[229]

On February 6, 1928, General Morfin and the Cristeros ambushed the Federales between Cotija and Jiquilpan. José rode at the general's side. The Federales overwhelmed the Cristeros in a bloody battle. As the Cristeros began to retreat, the Federales opened machine gun fire on them, hitting the general's horse. José watched as the horse dropped dead beneath the general and rushed over to him.[230] "General!" he shouted. "Take my mount and escape to safety. You are of far greater importance to the Cristero cause than I am."[231]

The general accepted José's heroic sacrifice. At once, José helped the general into the saddle and then swatted the horse's backside, sending it galloping away. After saving the general, José did not run to try to save himself. Instead, he took cover behind a rock and shot at the Federales, helping more of his fellow Cristeros flee. When José ran out of ammunition, he stood up and shouted, "I have not surrendered. I have only stopped shooting you because I am out of cartridges."[232]

The Federales were furious to learn it was a boy who had been shooting at them. They grabbed José, beat him, uttered blasphemies at him, and dragged him to a prison in Cotija. Another young boy, Lorenzo, was captured as well and accompanied José to prison.

That day, José wrote a letter to his mother:

Dear Mama,

I was taken prisoner during the fighting today. I think that now I am going to die. But that doesn't matter at all, Mama. Please accept God's will. I die very happy because I die on the battlefield right next to Our Lord.

Don't let yourself be distraught by my death because that would only upset me more. Rather, tell my other brothers to follow the example of the littlest one, and you just do God's will. Be strong and please send me your blessing, together with my dad's.

Say goodbye to everyone for me for the last time. And finally, accept all the love of your son who misses you so much already and wants to see you so much before he dies.

José[233]

The following day, the Federales transferred José and Lorenzo to a makeshift prison in his hometown of Sahuayo: his parish church, the Church of Saint James the Apostle, where he had received the sacraments of Christian initiation and attended Mass with his family. But this was not a joyful homecoming. The Federales had desecrated God's house, using it as a barn for horses and roosters and a depository for horse manure, food scraps, beer bottles, and military supplies.[234] It pierced José's heart to see the once-beautiful sanctuary vandalized by the now-powerful enemies of God and His mother—the beautiful Lady who had offered Her personal love to the people of Mexico and the world.

José was imprisoned in the church bapistry. A barred window looking out to the street gave José contact with the people of his town. They heard him praying and singing, "To Heaven, to Heaven, to Heaven I want to go." His family and friends visited him and even passed candy to him through the bars.[235]

The town had high hopes that one of José's visitors—Rafael Picazo, the mayor of Sahuayo and his godfather—would use his influence to have José released. Whatever loyalty Picazo may have felt to José and his family was not strong enough to tempt him to risk his good standing with the Calles regime. Picazo had dutifully complied with the Calles Law, showing his allegiance by denouncing the Faith and even changing the name of Tepeyac Street to Picazo Street.[236]

When Picazo visited José, he did so not as the boy's spiritual mentor but as Calles's underling and an apologist for his atheistic, anti-Catholic agenda. He told José he would release him if he renounced his faith. The Federales tried to convince José by beating him and depriving him of sleep and food, but their efforts were in vain. José never wavered in his fidelity to Christ. "I'd rather die than betray Christ and my country," he told them.[237]

Once, José's captors made him watch the hanging of one of his fellow Cristeros. The cruel tactic had the opposite effect, stirring in José a desire to comfort and strengthen the condemned man by assuring him of God's saving love. In the final moments of the man's life, José told him, "You will be in Heaven before me. Prepare a place for me. Tell Christ the King I shall be with him soon."[238]

Picazo tried another approach. He offered to help José attend military school and become an officer in the Federales. Offended, José told his godfather, "I'd rather die first! I will not go with those monkeys! Never with those persecutors of the Church! If you let me go, tomorrow I will return to the Cristeros! Viva Cristo Rey! Viva La Virgen de Guadalupe!"[239]

José remained strong for his friends and family and also for his fellow young captive, Lorenzo. José was a friend and counselor to Lorenzo. When Lorenzo became fearful, José spoke to his friend about Christ, Our Lady of Guadalupe, Anacleto González Flores, and Father Miguel Pro, another courageous martyr who had defended the Church against Her enemies in Mexico.[240] Together, emboldened by the love of God and His mother and the courage of their heroes in heaven, the boys remained strong.

Picazo was growing increasingly impatient with his godson. In an effort to break José down and force him into submission, he arranged to have José watch Lorenzo's execution. On February 8, soldiers prepared to hang Lorenzo from a tree in the main square. Instead of renouncing his faith, José encouraged Lorenzo to stay strong. He shouted, "Long live Christ the King!" and "Long live Our Lady of

Guadalupe!"[241] Amazingly, after the hanging, when Lorenzo's body was taken to the cemetery, the grave digger realized
the boy was still alive. He offered to bury the boy himself
so Lorenzo could escape, which he did, and was thereafter
known as "Lazarus" after the friend Jesus loved and raised
from the dead (see Jn 11:1–44).

That night, the guards released three roosters to fight for
sport in the church. The birds roamed freely and perched on
the tabernacle, the sacred dwelling for the Lord really present in the Most Blessed Sacrament. As soon as José saw what
was happening on the altar, he grabbed one of the roosters
and cracked its neck. One by one, he cracked the necks of
all the birds, shouting, "This is not a farmhouse!" "This is the
house of God!"[242] When José finished, he washed his hands
with a rag and prayed on his knees, devoutly and loudly.
Then he calmly went to bed.[243]

The next morning, Picazo was furious. He grabbed José
and screamed, "Do you know how much they were worth?"
José replied, "All I know is that my Father's house is a place
to pray, not to keep animals."[244]

Picazo punched him in the face and knocked out some of
his teeth.

José learned that he would be executed on the evening
of February 10, 1928. He notified his Aunt Maria in a letter, asking her to inform his mother because he could not
bring himself to tell her. He asked his aunt to say goodbye to
everyone for him. He ended the letter, "Christ lives, Christ
reigns, Christ rules. Long live Christ the King and Holy
Mary of Guadalupe!"[245]

At 8:00 p.m. that evening, his Aunt Magdalene smuggled the Eucharist to José, who was overjoyed to receive Jesus before he died.

At 11:00 p.m., under the cover of night, federal soldiers took José a block away to the army headquarters. There, they sheered the soles of his feet off, tied his arms around his back, and forced him to walk the rough and stony road to the cemetery, which was about a mile away. José's mother and a small group of relatives and friends followed him.[246] As he walked, he shouted loudly, "Viva Cristo Rey! Viva la Virgen de Guadalupe!" The soldiers were afraid he would wake up the sleeping town, so they tried to silence him by mocking him, stabbing him, and hitting him so hard with the butt of a gun that it broke his jaw. Several times, they promised to let him live if he would say, "Death to Christ the King." José screamed in pain, but kept shouting, "Viva Cristo Rey! Viva la Virgen de Guadalupe!"[247]

As devastated as his mother was, she encouraged him to remain true to Christ the King.

When the group arrived at the cemetery, the soldiers forced José to dig his own grave. They beat him, stabbed him, and dunked him in water until he almost drowned, all the while asking him to renounce his faith.

At 11:30 p.m., right before a soldier propelled a bullet through the fourteen-year-old's temple, ending the faithful, earthly life of heaven's newest occupant, José said for the last time, "Viva Cristo Rey! Viva la Virgen de Guadalupe!"[248]

Viva Cristo Rey

The townspeople and federal assassins were astounded by the faith-fueled courage exhibited by a boy so young, whose profound love for Jesus (his best friend) and for the Catholic Church (His Mystical Body) had so filled his human heart, he had become a witness to Saint Paul's complete abandon to Christ's will, as relayed in Galatians: "I have been crucified with Christ; it is no longer I who live, but Christ who lives in me; and the life I now live in the flesh I live by faith in the Son of God, who loved me and gave himself for me" (Gal 2:19–20).

In the hours following the boy's torture and murder, José's mother, assisted by a priest, recovered and buried her son's body. José's family and friends—those who remembered the boy's extraordinary devotion to Christ the King and His mother—visited his grave, as did many others who were inspired by his story (as José had visited the grave of Anacleto Gonzales Flores). One of José's assassins was frequently seen praying at José's resting place.[249]

In 1996, the remains of José's body were sent home to the Church of Saint James the Apostle in Sahuayo. That same year, the cause for canonization began. In 2004, Pope John Paul II declared that José was a martyr who died for Christ.

On November 20, 2005, Pope Benedict XVI beatified José along with eight other martyrs of the Mexican persecution, including one of his heroes, Anacleto González Flores.[250] Pope Francis proclaimed him a canonized saint on October 16, 2016, formally recognizing the holiness of the boy Cristero—the Mexican Tarcisius—who refused to give allegiance to the enemies of the Church who denied the eternal reign of Christ the King.

José's words to his mother, written the day he was captured by the federal soldiers, reveal a perfect understanding of the earthly duty of God's children who are destined for heaven: "Please accept God's will. . . . Tell my other brothers to follow the example of the littlest one, and you just do God's will."

Viva Cristo Rey.

Blessed Jerzy Popiełuszko

Jerzy Popiełuszko was born in a state built on lies—and lived his entire life under tyrannical rule. Yet he became one of history's most courageous truth-tellers. That's because he wasn't born into a *state*; he was born into a Catholic family who passed on the truth of the Faith—that all humans are born in the image and likeness of God for the purpose of loving Him and spending eternity with Him in heaven.

Jerzy knew from an early age that all people have dignity by virtue of their humanity. Inspired by his childhood hero, Saint Maximilian Kolbe, and two men who served as spiritual fathers to him, Cardinal Stefan Wyszyński and Pope John Paul II, he courageously proclaimed this truth, inspiring thousands of people worldwide to reject the lies of atheistic communism. He tirelessly preached the Gospel even as he knew his life was in danger. He was ultimately hunted down, tortured, and killed by government assassins, but as God's faithful servant, he did not suffer in vain. His brutal murder delivered him from the evils of this world and into the loving arms of his Savior in heaven. His story continues to motivate truth-seeking people throughout the world today.

A Formative Childhood

Jerzy was born in the village of Okopy, Poland, on September 14, 1947, on the feast of the Exaltation of the Cross. On this day, Catholics honor the holy cross on which Jesus Christ sacrificed his life to redeem the world. Jerzy's parents, Wladyslaw and Marianna Kalinowski, had no way of anticipating the significance of this feast day birthday—that the son they welcomed into the world would one day be called to imitate the redemptive suffering of Christ.

Okopy is a small village in northeastern Poland, in the Podlasie Province, near the town of Suchowola. Jerzy's family had lived there for generations. His parents were farmers who were accustomed to hardship and loss. They grieved the loss of Marianna's brother, Alfons—a soldier in the National Army who was killed by the Soviets in 1945—and a daughter named Jadwige, who died in Marianna's arms at the age of two on Christmas Eve in 1952.

Wladyslaw and Marianna worked long, hard hours in the fields. In fact, Marianna was working—she had left the house in the evening to milk the cows—when labor with Jerzy started. She managed to return home in time for her mother to deliver the baby. She said childbirth was not hard, but afterwards, she suffered from a bad headache and lost her eyesight for a few days, causing her to miss Jerzy's baptism.[251]

Jerzy was a small, frail baby. The family feared he would not live long, so they scheduled the baptism two days after he was born. He was baptized at the family's parish church in Suchowola in the name of Alfons. Marianna chose the name in honor of her brother and also Saint Alphonsus Liguori, a seventeenth-century Italian priest and Doctor of the Church. The family called the boy Alek—and that is how Jerzy was known, until he changed his name while in seminary.

Wladyslaw and Marianna gave their children a home life centered on Christ. They had a small chapel in their house and often prayed there as a family. They prayed on their knees every morning after waking and every evening before going to bed. They prayed to Our Lady of Perpetual Help on Wednesdays, to the Heart of Jesus Christ on Fridays, and to Our Lady of Częstochowa on Saturdays. They sang the Litany of Loreto in May and the Litany to the Sacred Blood of Christ in July. They prayed the Rosary in October. They abstained from meat on Wednesdays, Fridays, and Saturdays because, as Marianna explained, "man must know from childhood that renunciations are necessary in life, that not everything is like one wants."[252]

The Holy Mass became an integral part of Jerzy's life beginning in early childhood. His brother recalls that when Jerzy was eight or nine years old, he crafted an altar out of scraps of wood and spent a whole day imitating the gestures he had seen priests making at Mass many times.[253] He became an altar boy during his first years of primary school in 1954, serving Mass every day at 7:00 a.m. He had to leave his house at 6:00 a.m. to walk the three miles to the church in Suchowola. His mother said he made that journey every day, "no matter what season it was, whether it was raining or snowing or cold."[254]

Father Piotr Bozyk taught Jerzy his catechism. He was impressed with the young boy's zeal for his faith. He recalled, "You had the impression that he wanted to swallow in one gulp all the degrees of holiness."[255] The boy was religiously insatiable and appreciated the value of the interior life.

Marianna took seriously the responsibility to educate all of her children. She shared that once a parish priest said about Jerzy: "Mother, this boy may grow up to be the best or the worst man. Everything depends on your upbringing." Therefore, she explained, "I was trying to bring him up as best as possible. . . . Besides, the most important thing in life is to give God to children."[256]

The Popiełuszko children received a rich education at home that prepared them well for school and life. They read and listened to the Gospels and Polish literature, learning to love God and their homeland. They learned Polish history through their family's stories going back generations.

Polish History Passed on to the Popiełuszko Children

Poland had a long history of enduring devastating invasions by bordering powers. It lost its sovereignty for 123 years, suffering invasions and occupations by three neighboring imperial powers—Russia, Prussia (Germany), and Austria—which divided Poland among themselves in three partitions in the late eighteenth century. Having preserved its culture and national identity—in part through the persistence of Polish resistance movements—Poland regained its independence at the end of World War I in 1918. The Polish army heroically defended and protected its independence less than two years later, defeating an invasion by the Soviet Red Army in the Battle of Warsaw in 1920.

On August 23, 1939, Stalin and Hitler signed a "non-aggression" agreement establishing spheres of influence in Europe: Poland would be partitioned once again, with the Soviet Union taking the east and Germany taking the west. This part of the deal was kept secret so the invaders could manufacture reasons to justify their invasions to the world.

Mere days later, on September 1, 1939, Hitler's army invaded Poland from the west. To justify the attack, Nazi propagandists spread false accusations: that Poland had persecuted ethnic Germans living in Poland and was planning an attack on Germany with Great Britain and France. The Nazi Schutzstaffel (SS) and the German military even staged a phony Polish attack on a German radio station as the immediate pretext for the invasion.

Sixteen days after the Nazi army invaded Poland from the west, on September 17, 1939, Stalin's army invaded Poland from the east. The Soviets justified the attack by claiming they were coming to the aid of their "blood brothers," the Ukrainians and Belarusians, who had been trapped in territory that was "illegally" annexed by Poland when it regained its independence following World War I.[257]

Stalin immediately began rebuilding the Communist Party in Poland, which had been abolished in 1938 (due to the killing of most of the party's leaders and activists in Stalin's Great Purge in the 1930s). He established a puppet government in 1944—the Polish Committee of National

Liberation (the PKWN)—which was staffed by Polish communists and sponsored and controlled by the Soviet Union. The PKWN Manifesto condemned the Polish Constitution of 1935 as "fascist" and promised the rebuilding of the Polish (Russian-controlled) intelligentsia and universal, compulsory education.

The majority of the Polish people—including the Popiełuszkos—did not accept the PKWN as the governing body during the occupation; they supported the Polish Underground State, which was the union of resistance agencies that remained loyal to the Polish government-in-exile (located in London). Many men in Podlasie fought in the Home Army, the dominant resistance movement, during the war. Marianna's brother, Alfons Gniedziejko, was a lieutenant in the Home Army.

World War II lasted six years. It was the deadliest conflict in world history, resulting in seventy to eighty million fatalities.[258] Poland lost six million citizens, about one-fifth of its population;[259] this included three million Polish Jews—88 percent of its Jewish population[260]—and an estimated 20 percent of the Polish clergy—approximately 3,000 priests, sisters, and other religious, 1,992 of whom died in concentration camps.[261]

On January 4, 1945, the PKWN became the Provisional Government of the Republic of Poland, despite protests from the Polish-government-in-exile in London. In February, at the Yalta Conference, featuring the leaders of the United Kingdom, United States, and Soviet Union, Stalin argued that the Provisional Government should be made permanent. He said, "The Russians had sinned greatly against

Poland" and, in an effort to atone for those sins, the Soviet Union wanted to help create a "mighty, free and independent Poland."[262] United States president Franklin Delano Roosevelt and British prime minister Churchill agreed to recognize the Provisional Government as Poland's governing body, and Stalin agreed to allow free elections. Stalin, of course, had no intention of upholding his end of the bargain.

The Popiełuszko family was shaped by Poland's heroic resistance to evil invaders during World War II and the tyrannical Soviet abuses in its aftermath. Wladyslaw and Marianna were married in 1942. They had had their first child, Theresa, in 1943 and proceeded to have Jozef in 1945, Alfons (Jerzy) in 1947, Jadwige in 1948 (dying in 1952), and Stanislaw in 1954.

A week before the end of the war in Europe, on April 29, 1945, Marianna's brother, Alfons, died at the hands of the Soviets. This tragedy deepened the family's resolve to raise its children to love God and Poland and to always resist communism. "[The] children knew this history and understood what freedom of homeland meant," Marianna once said of Polish history, family history, and the heroic death of her brother, Alfons.[263]

As a boy and young man, Jerzy loved learning about the lives of the saints. His favorite saint was Maximilian Kolbe, a Franciscan friar who was martyred six years before Jerzy was born. He used to read *Knights of the Immaculata,* the Catholic newspaper founded by Father Kolbe, at his grandmother's house. His mom said this made him want to be a Franciscan when he was a boy. It may also be what liberated him from the fears of the world at a young age.

Saintly Inspiration: Saint Maximilian Kolbe

Raymond Kolbe—who would become Saint Maximilian Kolbe—was born on January 8, 1894, during the 123 years when Poland was occupied by three neighboring states. The Kolbe family lived in the Russian-controlled portion, first in Zdunska Wola, a small village near Lodz, and then in Pabianice. Raymond was one of five sons, two of whom died at a young age.

Raymond's parents—Julius Kolbe and Maria Dombrowska—were faithful Catholics. They were active members of the Third Order of Franciscans (now called Secular Franciscan Order), who joined religious communities after raising their sons. They cultivated in their sons a love of God and devotion to the Blessed Mother, praying the Angelus, the Litany of Loreto, and the Rosary every day.

Raymond became deeply devoted to the Blessed Mother at a young age. According to his mother, Maria, when he was ten years old, he prayed before a statue of Our Lady at their church, when, suddenly, she appeared to him. According to Maria, she held two crowns—a white crown signifying purity and a red crown signifying martyrdom—before Raymond and asked him to choose one. After some thought, he answered, "I choose both." The Blessed Mother smiled and disappeared—but stayed forever in the boy's heart.[264]

Also forever in young Raymond's heart was his beloved Poland. His father, Julius, was a patriot. He taught his sons Polish history and instilled in them a great longing for Poland's independence. After entrusting all three of his sons to the Franciscans—and becoming a part of the community himself for some time—Julius joined the Polish resistance to fight the Russian army for Poland's independence. Tragically, he was captured and hanged by the Russians in 1914.[265]

There was a time when Raymond thought he would serve Poland by enlisting in the military. But God had other plans for how to use this young man's extraordinary gifts to reclaim the rich heritage of his homeland.

Raymond was thirteen years old when he began his journey to the priesthood, entering a Franciscan seminary for minors with his brother, Francis, in Krakow. He received the Franciscan habit when he was sixteen and was given the name Maximilian after a third-century martyr who was killed for refusing to enlist in the Roman army. He made his final vows on November 1, 1914, All Saints Day. He was twenty.

Maximilian was recognized for his extraordinary intellectual gifts throughout his life. One of his closest friends, Bronislaus Strycznys, recalled how their teachers and fellow students "marveled at his deep and unusual grasp of mathematics."[266] He was one of seven seminarians chosen to study in Rome.

Maximilian thrived in the intellectual community in Rome. He was widely recognized for his genius in science, mathematics, philosophy, and theology. Not realizing the big plans God had for this humble servant, one of his teachers remarked, "It was a pity that he was going to be a priest because he had so many great talents."[267] Maximilian graduated *summa cum laude* with a doctorate in philosophy.

The year 1917 was consequential for the world, the Church, and for Maximilian. Three shepherd children in

Fatima, Portugal claimed that the Blessed Mother was appearing to them on the thirteenth of every month. They said she promised a miracle on October 13. That day, over seventy thousand people witnessed what is now known as the Miracle of the Sun; they saw the sun spin, change color, and nearly crash to the ground.[268] It had rained the morning of October 13 in Portugal. After the miracle, the field was dry.

One of the warnings Our Lady had shared with Lucia, the oldest child of Fatima, on July 13, 1917, was that Russia would spread its errors throughout the world, raising up wars and persecutions against the Church.[269] In October 1917, when the tyrants of the Bolshevik Revolution overthrew the Russian provisional government, they set out to destroy the Catholic Church. They seized all land and assets of the Church, including more than eleven million rubles which had been accumulated over centuries by the Church in the Polish-Lithuanian commonwealth,[270] forbade the Church to own property, and outlawed religious instruction in any school.

The year 1917 was also the two hundredth anniversary of the founding of the first Grand Lodge of Freemasonry.[271] Freemasonry is a seemingly altruistic, though secretive and deceptive, society, seeking "the destruction forever of Catholicism and even of the Christian idea."[272] In 1890, Pope Leo XIII warned that Freemasons were "possessed by the spirit of Satan, whose instrument they are."[273] He said Freemasons "burn like [Satan] with a deadly and implacable hatred of Jesus Christ and of His work"—and that they "endeavor by every means to overthrow and fetter it."[274]

As a young man, Maximilian was aware of the evil

unleashed into the world through the actions of unrepen-
tant sinners. But it was not until 1917, when he witnessed
the hatred of the Freemasons firsthand, that he realized God
was calling him to play a very special role in the spiritual
battle against the enemies of the Church. What Maximilian
witnessed was a celebration of the second centenary of Freemasonry in St. Peter's Square. He saw Freemasons holding
up signs that read: "Satan Must Reign in the Vatican. The
Pope Will Be His Slave."[275] He saw a black flag depicting
the Archangel Saint Michael under the feet of Lucifer. He
saw Freemasons evangelizing by handing out literature to
the people of the Holy City. He heard the vulgar chants of
the demonstrators:

> *Satan will rule in Peter's place;*
> *Popes and clerics become slaves*
> *To Hell's royal and robust race.*
> *He who preferred to reign in Hell*
> *Rather than in Heaven a servant be*
> *Will extend Hades' hegemony over his mortal*
>   *enemy—*
> *The Holy See.*[276]

An idea developed in Maximilian's imagination. He
wanted to fight evil by cultivating greater devotion to the
Blessed Mother, who "crushes the head of the serpent and
destroys its enormous body, made by all the various heresies
from many times and places."[277] In the summer of 1917, he
proposed the idea of forming a Militia of Mary Immaculate
to his superiors at the seminary. On October 17—four days

after Our Lady appeared in Fatima—Maximilian presided over the first meeting of the newly created Militia.

The goal of the Militia was to "win the whole world and every single soul over to [the Immaculate Mother], as soon as possible."[278] Each member would consecrate himself to the Immaculata "with no restrictions, that she [would] make full use of them as instruments for the work she herself undertakes, namely, to fight Satan and help souls in their sanctification."[279]

World War I ended in 1918, while Maximilian was still living in Rome. In the same year that Poland regained its independence, Maximilian was ordained a priest. A year later, Pope Benedict XV officially blessed the Militia of the Immaculata, and Maximilian returned to Krakow.[280]

The work of the Militia proceeded slowly at first. Then Father Maximilian had a radical idea about how to increase membership. Perhaps he was inspired, in part, by the Freemasons he saw distributing literature in front of the Vatican. The idea was to publish a newsletter. Many of his fellow friars mocked him, wondering how a Franciscan, who had taken a vow of poverty, would finance such an operation. But Father Maximilian was undeterred. Every day he prayed to the Blessed Mother. Step by step, he encountered the people he needed to help him finance, create, and publish the newspaper that would be called *Knight of the Immaculata*.

With the help of fellow friars—especially Father Alphonse (his younger brother, Joséph) who was a gifted writer and photographer—Father Maximilian published five thousand copies of the first issue of the *Knight* in 1922. Circulation grew steadily. In 1926, the friars published forty-five thousand copies and Maximilian went looking for a new printing location.[281] He found it twenty-six miles outside of Warsaw. It would become the location not only of the printing operation but also of the Franciscans' new friary.

On December 7, 1927, the eve of the feast of the Immaculate Conception, Father Maximilian and his Franciscan Brothers dedicated their new friary to the Blessed Mother. They called it Niepokalanow, which means "City of the Immaculata" in Polish. They began with Father Maximilian, Father Alphonse, and seventeen lay brothers and grew quickly. By 1938, it was the largest religious community in the world, with thirteen priests, 140 scholastics, and 609 lay brothers.[282]

Beginning in 1930, Father Maximilian spent six years growing the Militia of the Immaculata in Japan. He founded a second Franciscan friary in Nagasaki called the Mugenzai no Sono, which means "Garden of the Immaculata." Using Niepokalanow as a model, his friars published the *Knight of the Immaculata* in Japanese. Circulation increased steadily, reaching seventy thousand copies per year before World War II.[283]

Storm clouds were on the horizon, however. The 1930s saw the rise of tyrants who were hostile to the Catholic Church, especially Adolf Hitler in Germany and Joséf Stalin in the Soviet Union. Pope Pius XI responded with two encyclicals in 1937: *Divini Redemptoris* (Promise of a Divine Redeemer) expressed concern over the rise of communism in the Soviet Union, Spain, and Mexico, condemning it as "a system full of errors and sophisms" and "intrinsically wrong." He warned that "no one who would save Christian civilization may collaborate with it in any undertaking whatsoever."[284]

Mit Brennender Sorge ("With Burning Concern") was written in German, instead of the customary Latin. It was smuggled into Germany and delivered by hand to priests. It did not mention Hitler or the Nazis by name, but the target of Pope Pius XI's words were unmistakable. He wrote, "To hand over the moral law to man's subjective opinion, which changes with the times, instead of anchoring it in the holy will of the eternal God and His commandments, is to open wide every door to the forces of destruction. The resulting dereliction of the eternal principles of an objective morality, which educates conscience and ennobles every department and organization of life, is a sin against the destiny of a nation, a sin whose bitter fruit will poison future generations."[285]

In the meantime, Niepokalanow became home of the largest printing press in Central Europe. In addition to *Knight of the Immaculata*, which reached a circulation of nearly one million in 1939, the friars produced multiple other publications to further spread devotion to Christ through the Blessed Mother.[286] They even started a radio station to broadcast their message to a larger audience.

The media outlets of the Militia of the Immaculata were unapologetic vessels for the proclamation of truth in a world fraught with lies. They were anti-Nazi, anti-communist, and 100 percent supportive of the Catholic Church.

On August 23, 1939, the news reported the signing of a nonaggression pact between Germany and the Soviet Union. The friars asked how it was possible. Kolbe answered:

It's possible because the pact is directed against Poland. Two of the tyrants of our past history who kept our nation partitioned for more than a century now plan to divide our country once again. As your ancestors did, we must resist the destruction of our state. As they resisted the rule of Prussia and Russia, we must resist the rule of godless Bolshevism and the idols of an Aryan National Socialism.

Prepared for every sacrifice, let us entrust ourselves and our nation into the maternal care of the Immaculata, Poland's Queen. Beloved children, we can be confident that, if we do not survive the imminent storm, the Immaculata will not forget her people and her nation which fervently petition her.[287]

On September 1, 1939, the Nazis invaded Poland. Eighteen days later, on September 19, the Gestapo arrested all but two of the friars at Niepokalanow. What a terrifying experience this must have been for these men who had dedicated their lives to serving God. Father Maximilian comforted his brothers with these words upon their arrest: "Courage, my sons. Don't you see that we are leaving on a mission? They pay our fare in the bargain. What a piece of good luck! The thing to do now is to pray well in order to win as many souls as possible."[288]

This is how Father Maximilian understood his vocation: as a soul-winning adventure for Christ and the Immaculata. He spent three months ministering to the other prisoners at the Amtitz concentration camp until returning to Niepokalanow on December 8.[289]

On the feast of the Immaculate Conception in 1940, Father Maximilian published the first and only issue of *Knight of the Immaculata* during World War II. The issue contained Father Maximilian's final article, which included these powerful words: "No one in the world can alter the truth. All that we can do is seek it, find it, and live it. . . . If good consists in the love of God and springs from love, evil is substantially a negation of love."[290]

Fewer than six weeks later, the Gestapo arrested Father Maximilian, along with several other friars, for a final time. The arrest would lead to Father Maximilian's last "mission" at Auschwitz, where, in the presence of unimaginable evil and suffering, he would continue to call on the assistance of the Immaculata, "the predestined woman who was to crush the head of the accursed serpent."[291]

Father Maximilian was detained at the Pawiak prison before being transferred to Auschwitz. While he was there, an SS officer gave him the gift of being a witness of his faith to the other prisoners. Noticing Father Maximilian's habit, the officer approached him angrily, yanked his rosary off, and shouted at him: "Do you believe in this?!"[292] Father Maximilian answered calmly, "Yes, I believe."[293] The officer struck him in the face, drawing blood. Two more times, the officer asked the same question, and two more times, Father Maximilian calmly affirmed his belief in Christ, inviting the violence of the officer. When the incident was over, the other prisoners were upset, but Father Maximilian remained calm. He prayed and told them, "Everything for the Immaculata."[294]

On May 28, 1941, prison guards led Father Maximilian and 304 other prisoners onto cattle cars on a train headed to Auschwitz. Deprived of food and water, and forced to use a bucket as a toilet, the people huddled together in fearful anticipation of their arrival at the death camp. Father Maximilian approached the horrific train ride as he did all experiences in the world: he allowed the Immaculata to make "full use" of him.[295] Accordingly, he sang religious and patriotic songs, encouraging others to join him in affirmation of their God-given dignity.

When the train arrived at Auschwitz, the prisoners were stripped naked, forced to shower, sprayed with a disinfectant, shaved of all body hair, and given uniforms adorned with blue and grey stripes and, often, blood stains of previous victims; they were sorted and given triangular-shaped badges, worn on the left side of their shirts, to help guards identify them. Father Maximilian's badge was red with a "P" on it, identifying him as a Polish political prisoner.

As Father Maximilian looked out into the sea of prisoners held captive by Christ's enemies, it would not have been lost on him that they bore the traditional symbol of the Holy Trinity over their hearts; that the triangle that was meant to demean them—that was chosen to analogize "hazard" road signs in Germany—was a reminder of their innate dignity as humans made in God's image and likeness. Neither would it have been lost on him that he wore the color of one of the crowns he chose as a child.

Father Maximilian's days at Auschwitz were filled with hard labor, beatings, and gratuitous cruelty. But they were also filled with the joy of ministering to his fellow man through secret prayer, confessions, conversation, and friend-ship. Because even though he was a prisoner *of* the Nazis, he was, in the words of St. Paul, a "prisoner *for* the Lord" (Eph 4:1). The world had no claim on his heart. Satan had no claim on his soul. He was free to love as God loves.

On July 29, 1941, a Polish prisoner in Father Maximilian's cell block escaped, triggering a *Nazi Sippenjutiz*—a punish-ment calling for the execution of ten prisoners close to the escapee.[296] The next evening, after making six hundred pris-oners stand in attention in the summer heat all day, Deputy Commandant Karl Fritch and SS officer Gerhard Palitzsch began selecting prisoners to die the horrible death of being locked away in a starvation cell. They chose their victims one by one, walking through the crowd and pointing their batons at the terrified men, taunting some and condemning others to death. After selecting nine victims, Fritsch stood in front of a Polish army sergeant named Franciszek Gajown-iczek and told him to step forward. The devastated man cried out, "My poor wife, my poor children, who will take care of them?"[297] Fritsch beat him with an ox hide whip and the man continued to weep loudly for his family.

Deeply moved with pity for his brother in Christ, Father Maximilian made his way through the crowd. When Fritsch saw him, he yelled, "Back in line!" Father Maximilian con-tinued, causing Fritsch to take out his gun and yell, "What does this Polish pig want?"[298] Father Maximilian could have answered, "Eternal friendship with Christ." He could have quoted Jesus calling his disciples "friends" and revealing to them that "greater love has no man than this, that a man lay down his life for his friends" (Jn 15:13). Instead, he simply said that he wished to take the man's place because he was a Catholic priest with no family who was older and weaker (thus, less valuable as a camp laborer) than the other man. Fritsch paused for a moment. And then he agreed.

The guards led the ten men into an eight-by-eight-foot cell with a small window; it was empty except for a bucket that would serve as their toilet. The guards ordered them to remove all their clothing; then they locked them in the cell without food or water. Once again, Father Maximilian allowed the Immaculata to make "full use" of him. Centering the men's hearts on Christ, he prayed over them, quoted Scripture, sang hymns, heard their confessions, and comforted them in their last moments of life, cradling them in his arms and praying the Hail Mary as they died. After two weeks, four men were alive, but Father Maximilian was the only one who was conscious. The guards needed the cell cleared, so a physician at the camp injected the men with carbolic acid to stop their hearts. Father Maximilian—who once said "the most deadly poison of our time is indifference"—died almost immediately, freeing his soul from his tortured body as he joined His Savior and the Blessed Mother, the Immaculata, in heaven.[299] The date was August 14, 1941, the eve of the feast of the Assumption of the Virgin Mary.

Pope Paul VI beatified Father Maximilian in 1971. Pope John Paul II canonized him in 1982, saying these beautiful words at the canonization Mass: "And in this human death of his there was the clear witness borne to Christ: the witness borne in Christ to the dignity of man, to the sanctity of his life, and to the saving power of death in which the power of love is made manifest.[300]

More than 150,000 people attended Saint Maximilian Kolbe's canonization Mass, including Gajowniczek, who survived Auschwitz and spent the rest of his life speaking out about the evil of totalitarianism and the heroism of the saint who loved like Christ. By the time Gajowniczek died in 1995, he had brought Saint Maximilian Kolbe's inspiring example of moral courage to every country in Western Europe and to the United States.

Noticeably absent from the canonization Mass was Jerzy Popiełuszko. Jerzy had desperately wanted to be a part of the Church's celebration of his hero, but in 1982, forty-one years after Father Maximilian's death, Poland was not yet free.[301]

Calling to the Priesthood

When Marianna was pregnant with Jerzy, she prayed for the grace of a vocation for him, but she never told him. She raised her son in the Church and watched his faith mature throughout his childhood, even as pressures grew all around them to fall in line with communist expectations.

The year Jerzy was born was the same year the communist Ministry of National Education instituted a major overhaul of Poland's education plan.[302] Schooling for children would be government-controlled and compulsory: the same atheistic, Marxist curriculum would be taught at all schools throughout Poland, and parents would be imprisoned if they did not hand their children over to be uniformed and indoctrinated. The goal was to achieve a society of compliant individuals, loyal to the state above all else, dutifully performing their work as cogs in the collectivist wheel.

The people of Podlasie largely resisted the communists' re-education efforts. A network of faithful families, priests, and educators helped preserve Polish history and culture for young people. They passed on stories, read Polish literature and poetry, and practiced their Catholic faith. So, for example, when school history books taught that members of the Polish government-in-exile during World War II were traitors—or omitted Poland's victory in 1920 over the Soviet Union in the Battle of Warsaw as if it never happened—children could identify the lies.

Marianna recalled once being called into school about Jerzy; she was surprised to hear from the teacher because her son was a good student. When she met with the teacher, she learned it wasn't Jerzy's schoolwork the teacher was worried about, but his Catholic faith. The teacher told Marianna that her son attended church too often and would receive a lower mark on his behavior if he continued. Marianna's response was not to apologize or agree to restrict Jerzy's Mass attendance. Rather, she boldly informed the teacher that Poland had freedom of religion.[303]

While it is true that Catholicism was not outlawed—authorities believed it was too risky to attempt an outright ban—it was well-known that faith in God was antithetical to the communists' goal of achieving an atheistic society. Neither Jerzy's family nor his secondary school teachers, fortunately, shared this disordered goal.

Beginning in 1961, when he was fourteen years old, Jerzy attended a secondary boarding school in Suchowola that supported his growth as a faithful, well-formed Catholic. A young priest named Fr. Kazimierz Wilczewski had founded the school in 1945, right before the communists took over Polish education. Father Wilczewski hired teachers who were well-educated Catholics who were trained to teach in the Catholic and Polish tradition. The school had an excellent reputation for offering an academic program on par with the best schools in the country. An unusually high proportion of its students went on to university.[304]

It was at Father Wilczewski's school that Jerzy's zeal for the pursuit of truth emerged. Jerzy enthusiastically studied the lives of the saints and the history of the Church in Poland. His favorite works were books about Maximilian Kolbe and a collection of sermons by Cardinal Stefan Wyszyński. He became known as "the philosopher" because of his habit of grappling with the moral and ethical dimensions of all human actions.

In the spring of 1964, a few months before his eighteenth birthday, Jerzy told his mother that he was going to visit Niepokalanow, the Franciscan friary in Teresin that was founded by Maximilian Kolbe. Marianna understood that this meant her prayers had been answered: her son had a calling and would be a priest.

Jerzy visited the friary. Then he traveled east to the Seminary of John the Baptist in Warsaw, where he applied for admission for the next year. When he returned home, Father Porczyk tried to convince him to enter local seminary at Bialystok. But Jerzy had made up his mind. He would study for the priesthood under the direction of the staunch anti-communist whose words had already so deeply shaped his understanding of the world.

The rector of the seminary in Warsaw was Cardinal Stefan Wyszyński.

SAINTLY INSPIRATION:
BLESSED STEFAN WYSZYŃSKI

Stefan Wyszyński was born on August 3, 1901, in the Russian-occupied Polish village of Zuzela. He was the second of five children of faithful Catholic parents, Stanislaw and Julianna. The family spent a lot of time at their local parish because Stanislaw was an organist there. They prayed the Rosary together as a family at home. Stefan knew he had a vocation at a very young age, even before his mother tragically died when he was nine years old. It was a loss that deepened young Stefan's love for the Blessed Mother, which was already strong because of his upbringing.

The Wyszyński family resisted the Russification of Poland—the effort by Czarist Russia to strip Poland of its cultural heritage and replace it with Russian language, religion (Russian Orthodoxy), and culture. Russia was not subtle in its attempts to destroy the Polish identity. In the nineteenth century, Russia took over the schools, imposing a Russian education on Polish children. By the 1880s, schools were fully Russian; teachers even spoke Russian when they taught. In response, the Polish people began establishing a secret network of schools to teach children Polish history, Polish literature, and Catholicism—all in the Polish language;

the secret education system covered almost one-third of the country's population by the time Stefan was born. In addition, Polish parents became more intentional about passing on their Polish heritage at home.

Stefan attended a Russian-language elementary school, but his parents were patriotic supporters of the Polish resistance. They spoke Polish at home and read Polish literature. Stanislaw taught Polish history to his children. It was a tradition Stefan would continue decades later when, as a spiritual father, he would teach the Polish people to resist atheistic communism by reminding them of their Christian roots.

Stefan enrolled at the Pius X Lyceum minor seminary in Włocławek in 1917. Poland regained its independence the following year. He was ordained a priest six years later, in 1924, when he was twenty-three. He studied at the Catholic University of Lublin and earned his doctorate in 1929.

Father Wyszyński spent the six years of World War II observing the brutality of both the Nazis and the Soviets that resulted in the death of 6 million Polish citizens. This included 3 million Polish Jews and 800,000 ethnic Poles who were victims of the Nazi Holocaust,[305] and 150,000 Poles who died by Soviet executions (22,000 Polish officers in the Katyn massacre of 1940), imprisonment, and repression.[306] In addition, the Nazis deported 2.8 million Polish citizens for forced labor in German territories.[307] The Soviets arrested, conscripted, or deported 1 million Polish citizens, including 320,000 who were deported to Siberia.[308]

Influenced by the horrific killings and indifference to human suffering that he witnessed during the war, Father Wyszyński began developing a body of work based on what he called the "theology of the nation." He proposed that a nation is a natural community possessing natural rights from God[309] and that the state has a duty to protect these rights; the failure to do so rendered the state unjust and in violation of God's law. This is a message that would resonate deeply with the Polish people—especially a young Jerzy Popiełuszko considering a vocation to the priesthood. In 1942, Father Wyszyński wrote, "Inviolable human rights are prior to and older than anyone else's rights, both those of the family, the nation, and the state. They are independent of any social, economic or political system, and a system which would violate these goals will be unjust and slave-like."[310]

For nearly two years, the Nazis and Soviets honored the terms of their August 23, 1939, non-aggression agreement, which enabled them to pursue their own goals in Europe without fighting each other. That ended when the Nazis attacked the Red Army in 1941, causing the Soviets to align with Great Britain and the other Allied powers. This put the Soviet Union and Poland on the same side of the war. But the countries had different post-war goals. Poland wanted independence; the Soviet Union wanted a communist client state.

The competing post-war goals of Poland and the Soviet Union came to a head on August 1, 1944, when the Polish Home Army led a valiant operation—called the Warsaw Uprising—to liberate Warsaw from German occupation in assistance to the Allied cause. Despite pleading by Winston Churchill, Stalin not only refused to assist the Polish revolt but also prevented British and American pilots from refueling in the Soviet Union after airlifting supplies to the Poles.

The Nazis were ruthless in their response. During the sixty-three-day battle, they terrorized the people of Warsaw, executing Polish civilians in their homes, murdering doctors and patients in hospitals, and dousing wounded soldiers with gasoline and setting them on fire to burn alive—all with the Soviet army less than fifteen miles away. Poland lost thousands of the most courageous members of its resistance: between 150,000 and 200,000 Polish citizens died,[311] including 20,000 soldiers of the Home Army.[312]

Father Wyszyński witnessed the heroism and devastation of the Warsaw Uprising up close. Using the pseudonym "Radwan II"—he was wanted by the Nazis because he was a well-known and influential priest—he became chaplain of the Home Army's hospital in Laski and military district in Zoliborz.

The Polish people had hoped the end of World War II would bring independence. Therefore, it was devastating when, as the result of the Yalta Conference and despite the Soviet's horrific crimes against the Polish people, Great Britain and the United States agreed to recognize the Soviet-installed government as the official government of Poland, over the Polish government-in-exile. Then came another blow: the communist Polish secret police arrested most of the remaining soldiers of the Home Army on manufactured accusations of fascism and other charges. Many were executed or sent to the Soviet Gulags.

Poland had suffered the loss of many of its cultural leaders, including 18 percent of its Catholic clergy.[313] Pope Pius XII knew that Poland needed strong leadership. He appointed Father Wyszyński a bishop in 1946, primate of Poland in

1948, and a cardinal in 1953. As primate of Poland, in 1950, Bishop Wyszyński negotiated an agreement with the communist government guaranteeing certain basic rights of the Polish Catholic Church. The communists failed to keep their end of the agreement and instead embarked on an intimidation campaign designed to crush and control Church leadership. They arrested priests and religious, removed religion from schools, censored and sabotaged distribution of the Catholic press, demanded priests pay excessive taxes, imposed limitations on seminaries (for example, stopped allowing seminaries to award high school diplomas), and seized and liquidated monasteries, minor seminaries, and Catholic kindergartens.[314] They interfered in Church matters, prohibited the Church from publishing letters on "political matters," and ordered priests to spread communist propaganda. For example, Minister Bida ordered Fr. Antoni Marchewka of Częstochowa, editor of the magazine *Sunday*, to condemn the Nazis for the Katyn massacre,[315] despite knowing that the Soviets were responsible.

Cardinal Wyszyński refused to allow the Church to be used for unholy purposes. On the feast of the Assumption in 1952, he preached at Częstochowa, encouraging the Polish people to defend their God-given rights in pursuit of not only justice but also "domestic peace." He said:

> Let us remind others of the human rights: the right of life and a livelihood, the right to God, the right to truth, the right to love. Let us remind others of family rights: the right to freedom, to the choice of life, to a vocation; the right to domestic peace, the right to

property, the right to raise children and to a choice of schools.

Let us remind others of the rights of the nation: the right to a free country, to fidelity to country, to a place in our country, to history, language, and culture.

Finally, the synthesis and protective force of these rights: the Church, upon which is grounded the European culture that depends on the protection of these rights derived from Christ. The Church has the right to proclaim the Gospel from the pulpit, in the press, in books. The Church has the right to educational freedom and to Catholic schools! . . .

The defense of these rights leads to domestic peace. Whoever defends these rights renders a service to order and social success.[316]

The government doubled down. On February 9, it issued a decree claiming the right to approve Church appointments. Soon after, authorities began demanding the removal of priests from their posts. At the same time, attacks on the Catholic press increased: censors demanded editorial control and seized entire issues, preventing the Polish people from receiving unfiltered messages directly from the Church.

On May 8, 1953, on the feast of Saint Stanisław—the bishop of Kraków who was martyred by the king in 1079—Cardinal Wyszyński led the bishops in issuing a statement called "*Non possumus*," which meant, "We cannot permit it." The statement criticized the communist government for attempting to control the appointment of bishops, among other violations of the rights of the Church.

The communist government retaliated by arresting and imprisoning priests. Cardinal Wyszyński was imprisoned for three years without a trial. The time in captivity ended up being a great blessing for the Polish people. Cardinal Wyszyński used this time in contemplative prayer, planning a spiritual renewal for his beloved country. By the time he was released from prison on October 26, 1956, he had launched what would be known as the Great Novena—a nine-year prayer to prepare the Polish people for the millennial celebration of Poland's founding.[317]

Poland was founded on April 14, 966—the date of the Christian baptism of the first ruler of Poland, Mieszko I. Poland's founding is inextricably linked to its Christian roots. In fact, most Poles refer to their country's founding as the Baptism of Poland.

The Great Novena facilitated nine years of huge religious celebrations—bringing together Catholic clergy and Polish citizens—in towns and cities throughout Poland. Every event strengthened Poland's identity as a Catholic nation, thus undermining attempts by the government to Sovietize the people.

On May 3, 1966, Cardinal Wyszyński celebrated the Mass for the Millennium before an audience of half a million Poles.[318] Pope Paul VI had been invited to attend—and had accepted the invitation—but the communist government interfered, forbidding the visit. Cardinal Wyszyński made sure the Mass served as a reminder of the communist government's attempts to de-Christianize the Polish people: he placed an empty throne in the sanctuary and adorned it with a portrait of Pope Paul VI and a bouquet of white and yellow roses.[319]

The communists attempted to hijack the millennial celebrations. For example, they scheduled a parade on the anniversary of the signing of the communist PKWN Manifesto. But the propaganda efforts had the opposite effect; they were so transparently built on lies that they allowed the truth of the Church's celebrations—and the truth of the Faith itself—to shine more brightly.

Cardinal Wyszyński had succeeded in renewing his country's love of the people's Catholic Polish heritage. For this, he would be affectionately known as the Primate of the Millennium—a title the Polish people still use to refer to this titan of the Faith today. The importance of this feat cannot be overstated. When a Polish son and spiritual son of Cardinal Wyszyński, Cardinal Karol Wojtyla, became the first Polish pope, Polish Communist Party leader Edward Gierek realized that it was "impossible" not to allow the papal visit. Gierek was being pressured by Cardinal Wyszyński to allow the visit and by Soviet party leader Leonid Brezhnev *not* to allow it.[320] Gierek did not want to say yes. But the Polish people had a renewed patriotism. They were ecstatic over the news of the first Polish vicar of Christ in their country's millennial year. Against Brezhnev's warnings, Gierek allowed Pope John Paul II to return to his homeland. The decision would seal Poland's fate as a country of people who would be faithful to God, not to a government built on lies.

On May 28, 1981, Stefan Cardinal Wyszyński died at age seventy-nine, fifteen days after the assassination attempt of Pope John Paul II and three months after Father Popiełuszko started celebrating his monthly Masses for the Fatherland. Father Popiełuszko often used his homilies to pass on insights of Cardinal Wyszyński and Pope John Paul II that were relevant to the struggles of the Polish people—insights that Father Popiełuszko first discovered when he read Cardinal Wyszyński's homilies when he was a teenager. Cardinal Wyszyński's influence is obvious in these powerful words of a homily Father Popiełuszko gave to an eager audience of Polish patriots a year before his death: "Freedom is a value that God has inscribed in man since his creation. Failure to respect this right is an act against the Creator himself. As children of God, we cannot be slaves."[321]

Becoming a Priest in an Atheistic State

Jerzy entered seminary in 1964, when he was seventeen, and was ordained a priest by Cardinal Wyszyński on May 28, 1972. What happened during those seven years was tremendously formative for the young man destined to awaken the Polish people to their birthright of freedom.

The first two years of Jerzy's education and training for the priesthood were the last two years of the Great Novena. After nine years of a nationwide celebration of Poland's Christian founding, Jerzy experienced the anniversary year—1966—fully immersed in the teachings of the Church, under Cardinal Wyszyński's courageous leadership. Jerzy's mother, Marianna, recalled, "My son told us about sermons preached by Primate Wyszyński on this occasion, about millennium celebrations at Jasna Gora monastery, and about the fact that the authorities did not allow for the arrival of Pope Paul VI in Poland."[322]

That same year, several days after he received the cassock—with the powerful words and actions of Cardinal Wyszyński fresh in his mind—Jerzy was forced to begin his two years of compulsory military service for the Polish state. The goal of requiring all young men to spend two of their most formative years being trained by the communist military was to create a compliant, Marxist-indoctrinated citizenry. But the goal was bigger for seminarians, especially in the aftermath of the Great Novena and millennium celebrations of the Baptism of Poland; the goal was to compel future leaders of the Polish Church to abandon their faith.

Jerzy was sent to a special unit for seminarians in Bartoszyce in northern Poland. There, the seminarians received a special mix of training that included unholy temptations, Marxist indoctrination, and harassment and torture.[323]

The tactics had the opposite effect on Jerzy, serving instead to develop a habit of resistance in a young man who had been inspired by the courageous acts of defiance of his heroes since he was a child. Praying was prohibited on the military base, but Jerzy prayed openly, even praying the Rosary out loud. His friend, Fr. Marion Janeus, recalled the soldiers ordering Jerzy to stop praying—to put away his prayer book, rosary, or holy pendant—and Jerzy refusing. "Most seminarians would have followed orders, but he protested, out loud, and with a clear message," said Father Marion.[324]

Jerzy's defiance earned him severe punishments. Irate soldiers often ordered him to stand at attention throughout the night—sometimes in the rain and snow and often barefoot.

One day, Jerzy had an encounter with a soldier that is reminiscent of Father Maximilian Kolbe's confrontation with the SS officer who yanked the rosary off his habit. Jerzy wore a medal of the Blessed Mother around his neck. An officer asked him whose image was on the medal. Jerzy said, calmly, "It is the Blessed Virgin, the Queen of Poland." The soldier ordered Jerzy to "trample" on the medal, threatening to "pulverize" him if he disobeyed. Jerzy refused. The soldier tried to yank the chain off Jerzy's neck, but the chain, like Jerzy, did not break. Jerzy remained calm. The soldiers beat him and threw him into solitary confinement for one month.

The beatings and other physical abuse took their toll on Jerzy. He spent the last year of his military service in and out of the hospital, before returning to seminary.

Saintly Inspiration: Pope John Paul II Visits His Homeland

On October 16, 1978, the world celebrated the unexpected election of Pope John Paul II, the first-ever Polish pope and the first non-Italian pope in 455 years. The Polish people received the news with jubilation. There were reports of bells ringing, vigils in churches, and tears of "great joy."[325] The response from the Soviet Union and the Polish communist government was ten days of absolute silence. Behind the scenes, the communists were trying to make sense of what a Polish pope would mean for their ability to rule as before. KGB head Yuri Andropov asked the chief KGB resident in Warsaw how he could possibly "allow" the election of a citizen of a socialist country as pope?[326] The response of Polish Communist Party leader Stanislaw Kania was more on point than he, an atheist, could have possibly understood. "Holy Mother of God," he said.[327]

The Polish people were transformed after Pope John Paul II's visit to his homeland in 1979. More than twelve million Poles gathered with their fellow countrymen to see and hear from the supreme pontiff, who knew their hearts because he had suffered the injustice of tyranny alongside them as a Polish son. He told an eager crowd in Warsaw on June 2, 1979: "To Poland the Church brought Christ, the key to understanding that great and fundamental reality that is man. For man cannot be fully understood without Christ. Or rather, man is incapable of understanding himself fully without Christ. He cannot understand who he is, nor what his true dignity is, nor what his vocation is, nor what his final end is. He cannot understand any of this without Christ."[328]

Pope John Paul II concluded his remarks with this powerful and patriotic statement:

> I cry—I who am a son of the land of Poland and who am also Pope John Paul II—I cry from all the depths of this Millennium, I cry on the vigil of Pentecost:
>> Let your Spirit descend.
>> Let your Spirit descend.
>> And renew the face of the earth, the face of this land.[329]

It was a call to action to resist the atheistic, communist government that had denied the Polish people their birthright: to live a Christian life ordered to God's will.

Sitting in one of the first rows was Fr. Jerzy Popiełuszko.

Marxism and Solidarity in Poland

Whereas the Polish nation was founded on Christianity—which was established by Jesus Christ—the Polish communist government was founded on Marxism—which was established by Karl Marx. Marx was a nineteenth-century atheist whose writings reveal a contempt for Christianity and a fascination with Satan. Before he wrote the *Communist Manifesto*, he professed this supernatural thought in a dark work of poetry:

> Heaven I've forfeited, I know it full well,
> My soul, once true to God, Is Chosen for
> Hell.[330]

Marx rejected Christianity's truths that God created man in his image and likeness, that men have certain rights and duties by virtue of their humanity, and that governments are made up of men who have a duty to protect the God-given rights of the people. Rather, Marx presented the inverse of truth: that man invented God in his image for the purpose of advancing earthly goals.[331] He called for "all" of history to be understood not as the expression of the human desire for God but as the actions of men bringing about "a continuous transformation of human nature." He claimed this "progress" was normal and good.

He intended to be the architect of future transformations. He imagined a world where revolutionaries would pursue a "classless society," elevating the interests of the state over the rights of man. In pursuit of this goal, he called for property to be seized and private property rights to be abolished, and for the government to own and control all major economic and cultural institutions, including factories, farms, media, transportation, and education. He asserted that, through force and control, people would be conditioned to comply with the new order of a Marxist world.

Marx's ideas have resulted in widespread poverty and human rights abuses everywhere they have been implemented. Twentieth-century Poland was no exception. Central planning was an indisputable economic disaster, creating massive inefficiencies, inflation, and crippling shortages of food and other essential items for the Polish people.

By the summer of 1980, Poland was in a deep economic recession. Emboldened by the support of Pope John Paul II, the Polish people had grown increasingly impatient with their suffering. When the government announced yet another significant price increase, they were ready to act. On July 10, workers in Lublin declared a strike. Then on August 14, a thirty-five-year-old electrician named Lech Wałęsa led the workers of the Lenin shipyard of Gdańsk in a strike that would attract the attention of the world. During the night of the fourteenth, he worked with representatives from twenty other factories to form a strike committee that would become known as the Solidarity union. On August 22, Pope John Paul II affirmed his support for the union in a letter to Cardinal Wyszyński. He mentioned the "difficult struggle of the Polish nation to assure its daily bread, social justice, and its inalienable right to a life of its own."[332]

A delegation of five workers from the Gdańsk shipyard went to see Cardinal Wyszyński. They said they needed a priest to say Mass for them in the factory during the strike.

Cardinal Wyszyński told his chaplain, Fr. Boleslaw Piasecki, to find a priest. Father Piasecki and the steel workers went to the Zoliborz parish of Saint Stanislaus Kostka, where they "bumped into" Father Jerzy. They told Father Jerzy why they were there. Father Jerzy immediately agreed to celebrate Mass for the workers.

When Father Jerzy prepared for that first Mass for the steel workers, his heart was troubled by the uncertainties he would face. He was thirty-two years old. He had only been a priest for eight years. "How would the workers receive me?" he wondered. He was anxious. Would he appear foolish? Awkward? Maybe. He walked into the shipyard anyway. Here are his reflections from that day: "And then at the gate I first began to feel astonished. The crowds of people—crying and smiling at the same time, and clapping. At first I thought there was someone important right behind me. But they were clapping for me—the first priest in the history of this plant to enter at the main gate. It then crossed my mind—that this applause was for the Church, which for the last 30 years had constantly knocked at the gates of the industrial plants. My earlier fears proved to be unfounded."[333]

Father Jerzy remained with the steel workers day and night. He celebrated Mass, heard confessions, listened to their troubles, and offered them hope. On August 31, Lech Wałęsa used a pen depicting Pope John Paul II to sign an agreement with the government that became known worldwide as the Gdańsk agreement. The agreement officially recognized Solidarity as the Soviet bloc's first independent trade union and acknowledged its right to strike.

Father Jerzy became the chaplain of Solidarity, ministering to the ten million (out of thirteen million Polish workers) who were members.[334] But Solidarity was much more than a workers' union; it was the Polish people's resistance movement against communism. And that's why the communist government sought to destroy it—first by assaulting Solidarity leaders, then by imposing food shortages and blaming Solidarity for causing them, and then by releasing criminals into the streets so that the Polish people, fearful for their safety, would desire the restoration of law and order.

On December 13, 1981, almost five hundred days after the signing of the Gdańsk agreement, the communist government declared martial law, arresting and detaining thousands of Solidarity members and supporters, including Lech Wałęsa. Father Jerzy attended the sham trials of the accused patriots. He was the only priest who regularly attended the trials. He sat with the families in the front row, where the judges could see him well. Each time a verdict was read, he stood up, turned his back to the judge, and recited the national anthem to the people in the courtroom. Following the pre-determined convictions, he ministered to the workers' families and helped provide food, medicine, and clothing for them.[335]

Resuming a Powerful Sacramental Tradition

In February 1982, Father Jerzy immersed himself in a patriotic tradition that originated during the occupation of Poland in the nineteenth century, was resumed during the Nazi and Soviet occupation during World War II, and continued through communist rule: he began celebrating Masses for the Fatherland. Held once a month at the church of Saint Stanislaus, the purpose of these Masses was to worship God, incorporating Polish history and traditions, in resistance to efforts to deprive the Polish people of their heritage.[336]

Thousands of Poles attended Father Jerzy's Masses for the Fatherland. Some Masses drew twenty thousand people. This included non-Catholics who came to hear unfiltered truths spoken with courage—and it also included operatives of the communist secret police. Father Jerzy often based his homilies on the writings of Cardinal Wyszyński and Pope John Paul II. He boldly told the truth about life under communism. He said that without freedom, the Polish people were slaves, and the communist state was illegitimate because it violated the dignity owed to all people as children of God.

Father Jerzy challenged the lies of Marxism head on. He said, "The prevalent policy is an absurd, stubborn attempt to take God away from people and to impose on them an ideology that has nothing in common with our Christian tradition. This programmed atheism, this struggle against God and all that is holy, is at the same time a struggle against human greatness and dignity; for man is great because he bears within himself the dignity of the children of God."[337]

Father Jerzy urged the Polish people to stand up for truth. He said, "Our duty as Christians is to abide in the truth, even if it costs dearly." One Polish citizen explained the popularity of Father Jerzy's sermons. She said, "His preaching enabled us to distinguish good and evil."[338]

Father Jerzy's courageous truth-telling reached far beyond

Warsaw, thanks to an effort reminiscent of Fr. Maximilian Kolbe's inspired dissemination of *Knights of the Immaculata*. Solidarity members and supporters recorded his homilies on a tape cassette; they transcribed his words and dispatched the audio through a clandestine network of freedom fighters. Throughout Poland and the Eastern bloc, underground newspapers published his words, and Radio Free Europe, the source of uncensored news for millions of people living under communist tyranny, broadcast his voice. Father Jerzy became known worldwide as the humble Polish priest exposing the lies of communism—unafraid in the belly of the communist beast.

Courage under Fire

Father Jerzy said his "weapons" were truth and love, and they were. But the humble priest would not have attracted the attention of the authorities—and the world—if he had not also possessed another critical virtue: courage.

The communists knew Father Jerzy was a threat to their power. They used various tactics to try to silence him. First, they tried to coerce the Church to act on their behalf; they presented the Warsaw Curia with several "crimes" regarding the "anti-state" character of the Masses for the Fatherland. When the Church refused to back down, they resorted to physical intimidation and character assassination. Security officers followed him constantly. Twice, they broke into his apartment. Twice, they doused his car with paint. In the middle of the night on December 13, 1982, they threw a bomb into the window of his apartment.

During one of the thirteen times he was apprehended and interrogated, they planted evidence in his apartment designed to implicate him as a terrorist: plastic explosives, dynamite with a detonator, four tear gas grenades, thirty-six pistol cartridges, fifteen thousand copies of illegal writings, Solidarity leaflets, and five tubes of printer's ink.[339] Then they slandered him in the press by accusing him of criminal activity. Using the same kind of Orwellian language used to discredit truth-tellers today, authorities called him an "extremist," a "political fanatic," and an "agitator."[340] They called his Masses "hate meetings" and "political rage sessions."[341] It was deeply unsettling for Father Jerzy to think that the lies told about him would be believed. This was perhaps the greatest test of his courage. He persevered.

Father Popiełuszko knew his life was in danger. His friends knew it too, which is why they urged him to seek safety at the Vatican. But Father Jerzy believed that God was working through him, so he continued to preach the truth of the Faith.

Brutal Murder of a Truth-Teller

On October 19, 1984, Father Popiełuszko traveled 259 kilometers to Bydgoszcz to celebrate a special Mass "for the working people." He was not feeling well; he had a bad cold and a fever. His friends tried to convince him to stay home, but he did not want to let down the people of the parish of the Polish Brother Martyrs. He left his house with his driver, Waldemar Chrostowski, at 9:30 a.m. They were stopped by police officers on the way and permitted to continue with their journey. Father Jerzy celebrated Mass at 6:00 p.m., then prayed the Sorrowful Mysteries of the Rosary with the people, then he and Chrostowski headed home.

Three security police officers followed the car. They ordered them to stop, but unlike the police officers from that morning, they did not let them go. They used a wooden club and their fists to beat Father Jerzy until he was unconscious. Then they tied him up, gagged him, and threw him into the trunk. They gagged and handcuffed Chrostowski, who escaped by throwing himself out of the moving car. He survived the impact and was able to tell others what had happened to his heroic and holy friend.[342]

The media reported the abduction the next day. Immediately, people gathered at Saint Stanislaus Kostka Church for a ten-day vigil. Some people spent all their free time and every night praying at the church. On October 30, 1984, Father Jerzy's body was found in the Vistula River; his face was deformed from the violence of the beatings.

Truth, Love, Courage—and Eternity in Heaven

Father Jerzy said, "Fear is the greatest failing of an apostle; it restricts the heart and contracts the throat. Someone who remains silent about the enemies of the good cause emboldens them."[343]

Father Jerzy did not remain silent; he preached the truth of Christianity and its incompatibility with communism. He was harassed and brutally murdered for speaking out. But that is not the end of Father Jerzy's story.

Pope Benedict XVI beatified Fr. Jerzy Popiełuszko as a martyr on June 6, 2010, in Warsaw's Piłsudski Square—the location of Pope John Paul II's historic Mass during his nine-day visit to Poland in 1979. He called the martyrdom of the heroic priest a "special sign of the victory of good over evil."[344]

Jerzy's mother, Marianna, attended the beatification Mass. She was one hundred years old. In 2013, she offered this insight about her son's martyrdom and living the "good life": "Our life is in God's hands, and God knows what he is doing. In our life there is also suffering, but every suffering makes sense if you devote it to God. It is impossible to get to Heaven without the cross—he who is sowing in tears, he will reap in joy."[345]

Saint Teresa of Calcutta

Arguably, the most beloved human being of the twentieth century was not a head of state, titan of business, or rock star. She was a five-foot-tall religious sister who surrendered her will entirely to God. Now honored as one of the greatest saints of all time, Saint Teresa of Calcutta was known simply as Mother Teresa during her life. Her name is synonymous with goodness and charity.

Inspired by Saint Thérèse of Lisieux, Mother Teresa lived her life doing what she called "small things with great love." She founded the Missionaries of Charity, a congregation of sisters dedicated to serving "the poorest of the poor." Her work began in the slums of Calcutta, India, where she ministered to the sick and dying, and took her all over the world, where she confronted suffering in many forms. In the West, however, she discovered a different kind of poverty, a devastating spiritual poverty that could not be alleviated with medicine, food, or shelter. What the people in the West needed was God—but the people who needed Him most were those who were least willing to seek out His Word.

Mother Teresa's charitable work made her a celebrity. She was awarded the Nobel Peace Prize, invited to meet with world leaders, and asked to address internationally televised audiences. Time and time again, despite the harsh disapproval of many of the powerful elite, she used her platform as a do-gooder to advocate for the most vulnerable of the "poorest of the poor": babies in the womb in nations that permit abortion. Over the course of decades of her public ministry, she never diluted her message to make her hosts feel comfortable. She couldn't; she had made a promise to God many years earlier that she would never deny Him anything.

A Childhood Shaped by Christian Charity

On August 26, 1910, Nikola and Dranafile Bojaxhiu, a married Albanian couple, gave birth to Agnes Gonxha Bojaxhiu, the youngest of their three children, in Skopje, which today is the capital of North Macedonia, but at the time was part of the Ottoman Empire.[346] They baptized their new daughter the next day, giving her "God's most beautiful and magnificent gift"[347] of incorporating her into the Catholic Church.

The Bojaxhiu family had been Catholic, living as a religious minority for generations. Most Albanians were Muslim, and Skopje was becoming increasingly atheistic. Nikola and Drana were intentional about cultivating a deep love for Jesus and the Blessed Mother among their children. They prayed every evening and were heavily involved in the life of their parish church, which was named after the Sacred Heart of Jesus. They attended Mass regularly and participated in an annual pilgrimage to the chapel of the Madonna of Letnice in Kosovo. Agnes and her older sister, Aga, sang in the church choir.[348]

Nikola and Drana weaved charitable acts into the daily life of their family. They frequently opened their home to provide nourishment and companionship for less fortunate members of their community. Nikola used these moments as teaching opportunities. He instructed his children to "never eat a single mouthful" unless they were sharing it with others and to always treat their guests "warmly, with love."[349]

Agnes's brother Lazar described their childhood as "peaceful and pleasant."[350] Her father, Nikola, was a merchant and entrepreneur who owned real estate, supplied medicines for local doctors, and traded in oil, sugar, leather, cloth, and other goods. He took a keen interest in his children's education, was a talented storyteller, and was politically active. It was his concern for the future of his nation that may have caused his death when he was only forty-five years old. In 1919, he traveled 160 miles to Belgrade to attend a political gathering in support of the Albanian independence movement. He returned home hemorrhaging severely. Efforts to save his life failed. Members of his family and the medical profession were convinced he was poisoned.[351]

Agnes was only eight years old when her father died. She and her siblings were left in the sole care of their loving mother, who set up a business selling cloth and embroidery to support her family.[352] Even as a widow, Drana continued to live her faith by loving the less fortunate members of their community. At least once a week, she helped an old woman who had been abandoned by her family; she visited her, brought her food, and cleaned her house. Through deed and word, she instructed her children, "When you do good, do it quietly, as if you were throwing a stone into the sea."[353]

At the age of twelve, Agnes felt God calling her to religious life. She prayed about her future. Sometimes she doubted that she had a vocation. As a teenager, she joined a youth group for girls at her church called Sodality of Children of Mary. It was there that a Croatian Jesuit priest, Father Jambrekovic, introduced her to Saint Ignatius of Loyola's *Spiritual Exercises* and the missionary work of the Society of Jesus. By her eighteenth birthday, she was confident that God was calling her to be a missionary.[354]

In 1928, Agnes joined the Loreto Order, an Irish community of nuns. She traveled by train to Paris, where she received her postulant's cap. She spent six weeks learning English, after which time she set sail for India, where she would join the Loreto House in Calcutta in their education and humanitarian ministry.

As a postulant, she was no longer known as "Agnes" but "Sister Mary Teresa of the Child Jesus." She had chosen her name in honor of Saint Thérèse of Lisieux.

Saintly Inspiration:
Saint Thérèse of Lisieux

Born on January 2, 1873 in Alençon, France, Marie Francoise Thérèse was the ninth and last child born to devout Catholic parents, Louis and Zelie Martin. Louis and Zelie had both hoped to enter religious life and were initially disappointed—and then surprised and delighted—to discover they had a vocation of marriage and parenthood. "We must be open to generously accepting God's will, whatever it may be, because it will always be what's best for us,"[355] Zelie once wrote, conveying the full surrender to God that anchored her family's life.

Louis and Zelie experienced great joy as parents, but sorrow often cast a shadow on their happy home. Of their nine children, two sons and one daughter died as infants, and a daughter named Helene died at five years old. They named all seven of their daughters "Marie," after the Blessed Mother. They called the first "Marie" and the others by their middle names.[356]

By the time Thérèse was born, Louis and Zelie were mature and experienced parents. Louis was forty-nine years old and Zelie was forty-one years old. For thirteen years, they had raised daughters to love God above all else, to pursue holiness, and to understand heaven as the goal of their lives. As a result, Thérèse had four older sisters—Marie, her godmother, was thirteen, Pauline was twelve, Leonie was nine, and Celine was three—who modeled virtue and sanctity for her as she grew up.

Thérèse's early years were filled with love and happiness. She recalled, "My first recollections are of loving smiles and tender caresses; but if He made others love me so much, He made me love them too."[357]

Thérèse was surrounded by love from the moment of her birth. Louis called her his "Queen," and Zelie laughingly said her husband would do whatever their youngest daughter wanted. Zelie described Thérèse as a "child who delights us all," who was "very intelligent" and "extraordinarily outspoken." Her letters are full of stories of little Thérèse interacting with her parents and sisters in charming ways. For example, when Thérèse was nearly three, she asked her mother if she would go to heaven. Zelie told her, "Yes, if you are good." Thérèse responded, "Then if I am not good, will I go to Hell? Well, you know what I will do—I will fly to you in Heaven, and you will hold me tight in your arms, and how could God take me away then?"[358] Thérèse had full confidence in her mother's love and protection.

She also trusted fully in her older sisters' love and wisdom. When Thérèse was three years old, Marie gave each of her sisters a strand of sacrifice beads to encourage acts of self-denial. Zelie wrote that it was amusing to see her young daughter "put her hand in her pocket, time after time, to pull a bead along the string whenever she made a little sacrifice."[359]

Young Thérèse had a strong desire to please God, but she struggled to subordinate her emotions to her intellect and will. She was sensitive and high-strung, possessing a stubbornness that was "almost unconquerable."[360] She even threw "frightful tantrums" when she did not get her way.

When she was four and a half years old, Thérèse suffered a devastating loss: her beloved mother died from breast cancer at only forty-five years old. On the day of her mother's funeral, Thérèse threw herself into the loving arms of her sister, Pauline, and declared that she would be her mother from then on. Pauline obliged, acting as a second mother to her fragile little sister.

But Thérèse would never be the same. Losing her mother changed her, enabling her sensitive nature to completely overcome her naturally happy disposition. She wrote, "Instead of being lively and demonstrative as I had been, I became timid, shy, and extremely sensitive; a look was enough to make me burst into tears."

Three months after her mother's death, her father moved the family away from the worldly influences and liberal ideas of Alençon[361] and settled in Lisieux to be near Zelie's brother's family. Marie, who was seventeen years old, became mistress of the household and supervised her sisters' upbringing.[362]

In Lisieux, one of Thérèse's greatest joys was accompanying her father on walks every afternoon to visit the Most Blessed Sacrament in one of the local churches. On their way, she often gave alms to beggars.

In 1882, when Thérèse was nine years old, she received news about her "second mother" that shattered her delicate spirit: Pauline would enter the Carmelite Monastery in Lisieux. Thérèse felt abandoned once again. She wrote years later, "How can I describe the anguish I suffered! In a flash I saw life spread out before me as it really is, full of sufferings and frequent partings, and I shed bitter tears. At that time, I did not know the joy of sacrifice; I was weak."[363]

Soon after learning Pauline's news, Thérèse felt a divine call to enter the Carmel herself. She confided in Pauline, who took her to see the mother prioress. Thérèse learned that she could not be received as a postulant until she was sixteen.

When Pauline entered Carmel on October 2, 1882, becoming Sister Agnes of Jesus, Thérèse suffered deeply and soon became seriously ill. Her condition worsened over the course of seven months. Her family, and especially Marie, was constantly by her side. In May, the month of Mary, her father gave Marie money and told her to write to have a novena of Masses said for a cure for his "poor little Queen"[364] at the shrine of Our Lady of Victories in Paris.

Thérèse's health deteriorated. On a Sunday during the novena, Thérèse cried out for Marie, and when Marie came to her, she did not recognize her. Deeply upset, Marie knelt in tears at the foot of the bed, turned toward the statue of Our Lady, and prayed "with the fervor of a mother who begs the life of her child and will not be refused."[365] Leonie and Celine joined Marie in prayer, and then Thérèse joined too. Thérèse recalled what happened next: "Suddenly the statue seemed to come to life and grow beautiful, with a divine beauty that I will never find words to describe. The expression of Our Lady's face was ineffably sweet, tender, and compassionate; but what touched me to the very depths of my soul was her gracious smile."[366] Thérèse was healed instantly.

A year later, when she was eleven years old, she completed the sacraments of Christian initiation. She said her First Holy Communion was "the most beautiful day of all the days of my life."[367] She cried tears of joy. When she made her second Communion, she was so overcome by "inexpressible sweetness" that she cried again as she repeated the words of Saint Paul to herself: "It is no longer I who live, but Christ who lives in me" (Gal 2:20).

Tears flowed from Thérèse's eyes easily—and not just when she was filled with the joy of God's love. She cried when she experienced great sorrow, such as when Marie followed Pauline into the Carmel, and when she felt anxious, disappointed, or foolish. Sometimes she cried over having cried. She knew her extreme sensitivity made her almost unbearable to the people she loved.

On Christmas Day, 1886, when she was thirteen years old, Thérèse finally freed herself from her servitude to her emotions. When the family returned from Mass, she overheard her father sounding vexed, talking about her. He said she was too old to receive the babyish attention the family was accustomed to lavishing on her at Christmas. When Celine realized what was happening, she warned Thérèse not to show herself because she would "cry too much" if she opened her presents in front of their father just then.

This is the moment Jesus changed Thérèse's heart and helped her develop the strength of mind to love God selflessly and joyfully. Instead of crying, Thérèse surprised everyone when she happily opened her presents without a hint of the self-absorbed sensitivity they had come to expect from the beloved baby of the family. Thérèse reflected, "Love and a spirit of self-forgetfulness took possession of me, and from that time I was perfectly happy."[368]

Once free from the exhausting burden of disordered emotions, Thérèse was able to discern her vocation with an open heart and clear mind. One Sunday at Mass, part of a picture of the crucified Christ slipped out of her book, showing only His pierced and bleeding hands. Her heart was "torn with grief to see the Precious Blood falling to the ground and no one caring to treasure It as It fell." She recalled, "From that day the cry of my dying Savior—'I thirst'—sounded incessantly in my heart and kindled therein a burning zeal hitherto unknown to me. My one desire was to give my Beloved to drink; I felt myself consumed with thirst for souls, and

I longed at any cost to snatch sinners from the everlasting flames of Hell."[369]

Thérèse's desire to quench the thirst of Jesus increased day by day. By the time she was fifteen years old, her desire to enter the Carmel intensified. She felt called to contemplative religious life immediately. She obtained the consent of her father and uncle and was then told that the superior of the Carmelites would not allow her to enter until she was twenty-one. She and her father appealed to the superior and then to the bishop, who encouraged them to ask permission of the Holy Father on an upcoming diocesan pilgrimage to Rome.

Thérèse followed the bishop's advice. In a small private audience with Pope Leo XIII, after the vicar-general of Bayeux told them in a loud voice that they were absolutely forbidden to speak, Thérèse asked the Holy Father for his permission to enter the Carmel. He told her she would enter if it was God's will.

And it was. After returning home, Thérèse wrote to the bishop to ask for his answer. He gave his permission, which the Carmel received on December 28, 1887, the feast of the Holy Innocents. Thérèse entered the Carmel on April 9, 1888, on the feast of the Annunciation. She was given the name "Sister Thérèse of the Child Jesus."

Thérèse spent the remaining nine years of her life at the Carmel. During that time, she faithfully carried out her community responsibilities while discovering "a means of getting to Heaven by a little way—very short and very straight, a little way that is wholly new."[370] Her "little way," which she called "the way of spiritual childhood,"[371] was to do all things, every day, lovingly for God: "Miss no opportunity of making some small sacrifice, here by a smiling look, there by a kindly word; always doing the smallest right and doing it all for love." This is how Thérèse lived her short life in the monastery—smiling at others even when she didn't feel happy, doing chores pleasantly, and bearing annoyances without complaining. "We should go to the end of our strength before we complain,"[372] she explained.

Thérèse had tremendous admiration for the great saints— so much so, that she longed to be a martyr, missionary, and doctor of the Church.[373] It was a longing that only grew during her time at the Carmel. She did not set boundaries on what she was willing to offer God. Realizing that God desires fidelity in all moments, big and small, she committed to loving God fully moment to moment, which helped her avoid becoming overwhelmed or discouraged by past events or future anxieties.[374] Explaining her full surrender to God's will, she wrote, "My God, I choose everything—I will not be a saint by halves. I am not afraid of suffering for Thee; I fear only one thing, and that is to do my own will. Accept the offering of my will, for I choose all that Thou willest."[375]

Her full surrender allowed her to recognize that her goodness came not from her own merit but from the source of all goodness. "I know when I show charity to others," she wrote, "it is simply Jesus acting in me, and the more closely I am united to Him, the more dearly I love my Sisters."[376]

She was desperate to be a vessel from which Jesus's saving love could flow. Her concern for poor souls naturally extended beyond the physical and emotional to the spiritual needs of God's children. She told one of her sisters, "Had

I been rich, I could never have seen a poor person hungry without giving him [something] to eat. This is my way also in the spiritual life. There are many souls on the brink of Hell, and as my earnings come to hand they are scattered among these sinners. The time has never yet been when I could say, "'Now I am going to work for myself.'"377

She taught her "little way" to the novices entrusted to her care and to two missionary priests, Fr. Adolphe Roulland and Fr. Maurice Bellière, whom she supported with prayer and sacrifice. She engaged the young women in patient conversation and taught them original prayers and poems. She corresponded with the priests by letter. She considered herself to be the "little brush" that Jesus had chosen to "paint His Likeness" in the souls that had been confided to her care.378

On April 3, 1896, on the night between Holy Thursday and Good Friday, she coughed up blood, which was the first sign that she had contracted the deadly disease of tuberculous. By that time, Thérèse had been suffering joyfully, from one small moment to the next, for many years. Her "little way" had become a habit. It strengthened her, preparing her mind, body, and soul to suffer joyfully for Christ in the terrible moments that laid ahead.

For seventeen months, Thérèse's body was overtaken by the horrid disease. The last two months after she received Extreme Unction were especially brutal. But Thérèse had prepared well for this trial. She told her novices, "I have reached a point where I can no longer suffer, because all suffering has become so sweet."379 The doctor exclaimed to her sisters, "If you only knew what she has to endure! I have never seen anyone suffer so intensely with a look of supernatural joy. . . . I will not be able to cure her; she was not made for this earth."[380]

Thérèse died on September 30, 1897. Her last words were, "Oh! . . . I love Him! . . . My God, I . . . love . . . Thee!"[381]

One year after her death, Thérèse's autobiography, *Story of a Soul,* was published and distributed to a limited audience. Thérèse had started the manuscript when she was twenty-two; she contributed key additions during her illness, at which time her sisters also contributed memories. Among the wonderful revelations and autobiographical details in the book is this promise from Thérèse: "I will send down a shower of roses from the heavens; I will spend my heaven doing good upon earth."

Thérèse kept her promise. Devotion to the "Little Flower" spread throughout the world as *Story of a Soul* quickly became one of the most-read books of all time. Soon after her death, some of those praying for Thérèse's intercession were amazed to discover that Thérèse's "shower of roses" was more than a metaphor; when they prayed to Thérèse, they discovered roses as a sign that their prayers had been answered. Thérèse continues to delight God's children in this way today.

Pope Pius XI beatified Thérèse on August 29, 1923, dispensing with the customary fifty-year delay required between death and beatification. Pius XI canonized her on May 17, 1925, only twenty-eight years after her death. He proclaimed her universal patron of the missions, alongside Saint Francis Xavier, on December 14, 1927.

On October 19, 1998, Pope John Paul II declared her the thirty-third Doctor of the Church—the youngest person and one of only four women to receive such an honor. He described Saint Thérèse as the "authoritative teacher" of the overwhelming message of God's love.[382]

From Novice to Mother to a Life-Changing Promise

On May 23, 1929, Sister Teresa of the Child Jesus received the holy habit and was formally made a Loreto novice. During her novitiate, she received training to prepare her to serve the impoverished people of India. That training included language instruction in Hindi and Bengali. One of her sisters, Sister Marie Thérèse, remembered her at this time as a "great girl, very jolly and bright, full of fun," "very hard working," and "a very kind and charitable sort of person even as a young nun."[383]

On May 24, 1931, Sister Teresa took her first temporary vows and began teaching in the Loreto convent school in Darjeeling. For a brief period, she also assisted the nursing staff at a small medical station. These experiences provided her with her first encounters with the very poor people of India. She responded with extraordinary love and compassion, always putting Jesus at the center of her word.

At the medical station, a picture of Christ the Redeemer hung on the wall of the pharmacy. Every morning, before opening the door to catch her first glimpse of the sick people awaiting her care, she looked at the picture and thought, "Jesus, it is for you and for souls!" One day, a man brought her an emaciated boy on the brink of death. Filled with love of Christ and guided by his words, "Who so receives a child, receives me," she folded the boy in her apron. "The child has found a second mother," she declared.[384]

She did not stay in Darjeeling long. Her next assignment took her to several schools in Calcutta, including a primary school whose poverty-stricken pupils caused her to be "full of anguish." "It is not possible to find worse poverty," she wrote. It is here that she discovered the extraordinary power of love to spread joy even amidst extreme suffering. When she placed her hand on each dirty little head, the children showed extraordinary joy. "How little it takes to make simple souls happy!" she realized.[385]

On Monday, May 24, 1937, she took her final vows of poverty, chastity, and obedience. As was the custom for Loreto sisters, she became known as "Mother Teresa."

Mother Teresa began visiting the slums of Calcutta every Sunday. Because of her vow of poverty, the only material support she could offer were small and tattered items she found in her community that no one wanted. But her greatest gifts were not material. To those who felt abandoned, she gave her company in a spirit of friendship. To those yearning for hope, she gave the stories of the Gospels. One of Mother Teresa's pupils recalled that she frequently told the story of the Samaritan woman: "How Christ was thirsting for water, and how He is thirsting for love."[386] She also frequently told the story of the Visitation: "How Our Lady went in haste because charity cannot wait."[387]

It was not enough for Mother Teresa to know she loved the people she served. She was desperate for the people she served to know they were loved—by her and by God. She often spoke of the power of a smile to spread love. "The smile is the beginning of love," she explained.[388]

In 1942, Mother Teresa surrendered herself fully to love.

In a gesture reminiscent of Saint Thérèse of Lisieux's choosing "all that Thou willest," she privately vowed to refuse God nothing.[389]

Four years later, God asked for something big. On September 10, 1946, Mother Teresa was on a train to a spiritual retreat in Darjeeling when she experienced God's call to be a Missionary of Charity. "I was to leave the convent and help the poor while living among them," she recalled. "It was an order. To fail it would have been to break the faith."[390]

Answering God's Call

Mother Teresa formulated her plans for the Missionaries of Charity during the retreat in Darjeeling. The priest who directed the retreat noticed she was even more deeply immersed in prayer than usual. He also noticed she spent time scribbling notes on small slips of paper. Those notes contained the blueprints for a new congregation that would serve the "poorest of the poor" in a "spirit of poverty and cheerfulness"—not from a hospital or institution—but in the slums, "among those abandoned, those with nobody, the very poorest."[391]

In October of 1946, Mother Teresa shared her plans with Fr. Celeste Van Exem, a Belgian Jesuit who served as her spiritual director; it was a role he assumed reluctantly out of obedience to the archbishop. He initially considered his time with Mother Teresa to be a distraction from his "true vocation" of working with intellectuals. But he soon came to understand this simple nun's extraordinary "union with God" and he became an advocate for her.[392] The process revealed Mother Teresa's tenacity. She repeatedly persuaded Father Van Exem to visit the archbishop to encourage him to advance her request. "The Lord wants it now," she urged.[393] Finally, in January of 1948, the archbishop granted his permission to begin the application process. In the spring, the Propagation of the Faith granted permission for Mother Teresa to leave Loreto for one year to pursue her work and to continue after the first year with the archbishop's permission.

On August 16, 1947, Mother Teresa left the Loreto convent dressed not in the black habit she wore for nearly twenty years but in a white sari edged with three blue stripes. It was the least expensive fabric she could find and it appealed to her because blue was the color associated with the Blessed Mother.

Mother Teresa was now on her own. She found free lodging first with the Little Sisters of the Poor, a congregation committed to poverty and dependence on Divine Providence, and then with a local landowner. But she was no longer part of a religious community. Every day, she walked to the crowded slums to serve the immediate needs of the impoverished people she encountered. This included basic medical and humanitarian aid, all provided with love and good cheer. Within a few months, she gained permission to start a "school" in Motijhil. It was an outdoor space among the huts, where she taught children hygiene, the catechism, needlepoint, and reading; she also washed them if they were dirty.

Gradually, word spread about her one-person ministry. People gave her money and volunteered their time. Before long, she was able to rent two huts: one to be used for the school and the other for a home for the sick and dying.

Mother Teresa called the home a "resting place for people going to Heaven."[394]

On March 19, 1949, Subhasini Das, a Bengali girl who had been one of Mother Teresa's students at the Loreto convent school, became the first future novice of the Missionaries of Charities. The first ten young women to join Mother Teresa were all former students. Together, they worked in the slums every day, motivated by the message in Matthew's Gospel: "As you did it to one of the least of these my brethren, you did it to me" (Mt 25:40).

Mother Teresa taught the young women who joined her to see Jesus in every human being they encountered—and to satisfy His hunger for souls by satisfying the world's hunger for love. She explained:

> [Jesus] made himself the bread of life to satisfy our hunger for his love—our hunger for God—because we have been created for that love. We have been created in his image. We have been created to love and be loved and he has become man to make it possible for us to love as he loved us. He makes himself the hungry one, the naked one, the homeless one, the sick one, the one in prison, the lonely one, the unwanted one, and he says, "You did it to me." He is hungry for our love and this is the hunger of our poor people.[395]

In April 1950, Father Van Exem wrote a formal constitution for the Missionaries of Charity based on Mother Teresa's notes, which appear to be inspired by Saint Thérèse's words: "My one desire was to give my Beloved to drink; I felt myself consumed with thirst for souls, and I longed at any cost to snatch sinners from the everlasting flames of Hell."[396] Con-secrated to the Immaculate Heart of Mary, the aim of the new congregation would be to "quench the infinite thirst of Jesus Christ on the Cross for love of souls."[397] Sisters would serve "the poorest of the poor" in a spirit of "loving trust," "total surrender," and "cheerfulness."[398] Father Van Exem brought the constitution to Rome for approval. Pope Pius XII swiftly gave his endorsement.

On October 7, 1950, the eleven young women who had joined Mother Teresa became the first postulants of the Missionaries of Charity. On April 12, 1953, the first group of Missionary Sisters of Charity took their first vows of poverty, chastity, obedience, and "wholehearted free service to the poorest of the poor." Mother Teresa took her final vows as a Missionary of Charity in the same ceremony.[399]

Serving the Poorest of the Poor

Mother Teresa had fully surrendered her will to God. She had left her familiar and happy life at the Loreto convent with nothing more than her faith and the support of a once-reluctant spiritual director. Now, she was the founder of a religious community, inviting others to serve God by serving His children with deep intimacy, humility, and love.

By 1955, forty-eight young women had joined her as Missionary Sisters of Charity. She urged them to embrace their "beautiful vocation" with zeal and joy: "My very dear children, let us love Jesus with our whole heart and soul. Let us bring him many souls. Keep smiling. Smile at Jesus in your suffering—for to be a real Missionary of Charity you must be a cheerful victim. There is nothing special for you to do but to allow Jesus to live his life in you by accepting whatever he gives and giving whatever he takes with a big smile."[400]

Mother Teresa's love for the "poorest of the poor" could not be contained in the geographical boundaries of Calcutta. News of her good and holy work spread—and soon, bishops began inviting her to establish houses all over the world. First, she expanded to Bombay, India, then Cocorote, Venezuela, then Rome, Italy. By 1970, Missionary Sisters of Charity were on six continents: Asia (1950), South America (1965), Europe (1968), Africa (1968), Australia (1970), and North America (1970). By 1980, they were in seventy-four cities outside of India.[401] Jesus's words, "I thirst"—which had kindled a burning desire in the hearts of both Saint Thérèse and Mother Teresa to serve Christ in the world— were inscribed in all the congregation's chapels. It is a tradition that continues today.[402]

Mother Teresa brought her same generous spirit to the Missionaries of Charity houses throughout the world. But she discovered that all assignments were not the same. Because all poverty, while similarly devastating, is not the same.

It was Mother Teresa's first visit to London in the winter of 1970 that alerted her to the distinctive poverty of materially wealthy societies. The suffering people of London did not look like the suffering people of Calcutta; their bodies were not emaciated, scarred from smallpox, or infested with worms. They had access to clean water and adequate food to keep their bodies healthy. But the people still neglected, used, and abused each other and themselves. Mother Teresa walked the city streets and saw men and women sleeping outside, walking into strip clubs, and feeding addictions with drugs and alcohol. She even saw a well-dressed young man overdose on barbiturates right before her eyes. She observed, "Here you have the Welfare state. Nobody need starve. But there is a different poverty. The poverty of the spirit, of loneliness and being unwanted."[403]

She called this poverty a "spiritual poverty" and she spoke of it often throughout her ministry. Here is a story she shared about visiting a home for "old parents of sons and daughters":

> I went there, and I saw in that home they had everything, beautiful things, but everybody was looking toward the door. And I did not see a single one with a smile on their face. And I turned to the sister and I asked: "How is that? How is it that these people who have everything here, why are they all looking toward the door? Why are they not smiling?"
>
> I am so used to see the smiles on our people, even the dying ones smile. And she said: "This is nearly every day. They are expecting, they are hoping that a son or daughter will come to visit them. They are hurt because they are forgotten." And see—this is where love comes. That poverty comes right there in our own home, even neglect to love.[404]

Mother Teresa was moved with pity for the suffering souls of the world. She ministered to them, not just by doing charitable work, but also by using her influence as a trusted humanitarian to raise awareness about grave injustices and encouraging a loving response.

Something Beautiful for God

It was British journalist Malcolm Muggeridge who introduced Mother Teresa to the world. Muggeridge was known internationally as a bold truth-seeker. In the 1930s, he had helped expose Stalin's forced famine and starvation of millions of Ukrainians—a horrific human rights violation that other journalists had helped the communist dictator cover up. He served as a British soldier and spy during World War II. In the 1960s, he became a broadcast journalist for BBC television. Viewers came to expect his tough and critical approach to investigating and reporting the news. So when he chose to profile a humble nun, people paid attention.

In 1968, Muggeridge interviewed Mother Teresa for the BBC. At the time, her work was not well known outside of the Catholic Church.[405] Her humility made her reluctant to participate, but she consented out of a desire to bring her message of love in action—God's message—to a larger audience. When the interview aired, it was the first time members of the general public laid eyes on the simple nun who would become an international sensation. The interview was an enormous success, capturing the hearts of not just viewers but the interviewer too.

Muggeridge was deeply impressed with Mother Teresa. He wanted to see her work up close and share it with the world. He asked if he could bring a camera crew to Calcutta to create a documentary film about her work. Again, she was reluctant. And again, she consented, saying, "Let us then use the occasion to do something beautiful for God."[406] When the film aired on BBC in 1969, it was titled: *Something Beautiful for God.*

More recognition followed. On January 6, 1971, Pope Paul VI honored Mother Teresa as the first recipient of the Pope John XXIII Peace Prize.[407] On October 15, 1971, the Joseph P. Kennedy Jr. Foundation honored her with an award that bore these words: "To Mother Teresa, whose struggles have shaped something beautiful for God."[408]

In 1971, HarperCollins published Muggeridge's book about Mother Teresa under the fitting title *Something Beautiful for God.* The book, which described Mother Teresa as embodying "Christian love in action," was a huge success.[409] In it, Muggeridge offered, "It will be for posterity to decide whether she is a saint. I only say of her that in a dark time she is a burning and shining light; in a cruel time, a living embodiment of Christ's gospel of love; in a godless time, the Word dwelling among us, full of grace and truth. For this, all who have the inestimable privilege of knowing her, of knowing of her, must be eternally grateful."[410]

A growing number of people were becoming convinced of the importance of celebrating Mother Teresa's story. In 1972, several prominent figures submitted her name to the Norwegian Noble Committee for consideration for the award widely regarded to be the most prestigious in the world: the Nobel Peace Prize. Muggeridge was among her most ardent supporters. When the committee asked for more information about her work to promote peace, it was Muggeridge who answered. He recalled, "I tried to explain how, by dedicating her life wholly to Christ, by seeing in every suffering soul her Savior and treating them accordingly, by being, along with her Missionaries of Charity, a sort of power-house of love in the world, she was a counter-force to the power-mania, cupidity and egoistic pursuits, out of which violence, individual and collective, in all its forms, comes."[411]

The committee did not award her the prize that year, but Muggeridge and others continued to lobby for her candidacy for several years. In the meantime, she continued to be recognized around the world. In 1973, she became the first recipient of the Templeton Prize for Progress in Religion.[412] In 1975, she became the first recipient of the Albert Schweitzer International Prize for humanities.[413] In 1977, she was awarded an honorary doctorate in Theology from the University of Cambridge, England.[414]

On October 17, 1979, the committee announced its decision to award the Nobel Peace Prize to Mother Teresa "for her work for bringing help to suffering humanity."[415] The news was groundbreaking, marking the first and only time the prestigious award would go to a Catholic religious sister.

On the World's Stage

On December 10, 1979, Mother Teresa found herself with the most significant and far-reaching platform she had ever been offered. Two days earlier, she had arrived in Oslo, Norway, where thousands of dignitaries, notable guests, and members of the international press corps had come together to be a part of the events honoring her.

When she took the podium, she began by asking the audience to recite Saint Francis's *Prayer for Peace*. They had received cards with the words at their seats. Noting that the world's problems were the same then as they were in Saint Francis's day, she led many of the highest ranking and most influential people in the world in praying to God:

> Lord, make me a channel of your peace. . . .
> Lord, grant that I may seek [rather]. . . to
>   comfort than to be comforted . . .
> to love, than to be loved.
> For it is by forgetting self, that one finds . . .
> It is by dying, that one awakens to eternal
>   life.
> Amen.[416]

In humility, she accepted the award on behalf of "all those people who feel unwanted, unloved, uncared [for], thrown away [by] society, people who have become a burden to . . . society." She explained that God became man and asks us to see Him in each other: "He makes himself that hungry one, that naked one, that homeless one, not only hungry for bread, but hungry for love, not only naked for a piece of cloth, but naked of that human dignity, not only homeless for a room to live, but homeless for . . . being forgotten."

In other words, Jesus wants us to see Him in the poorest of the poor whom society forgets—those who deserve love and dignity by virtue of their humanity, whom society casts aside without regard to their humanity. Not only does He desire this of us; He requires it as a condition for salvation. As she reminded her distinguished audience, "He said that at the hour of death we are going to be judged on what we have been to the poor, to the hungry, naked, the homeless."

Nine minutes into her remarks, she made a plea in the name of world peace on behalf of millions of unborn babies who are victims of abortion. Passionately, she shared:

> And I feel one thing I want to share with you all, the greatest destroyer of peace today is the cry of the innocent unborn child. For if a mother can murder her own child in her own womb, what is left for you and for me to kill each other? Even in the scripture it is written: Even if mother could forget her child – I will not forget you – I have carved you in the palm of my hand. Even if mother could forget, but today millions of unborn children are being killed. And we say nothing. In the newspapers you read numbers of this one and that one being killed, this being destroyed, but nobody speaks of the millions of little ones who have been conceived to the same life as you and I, to the life of God, and we say nothing, we allow it.

And then she got really bold: "To me the nations who have legalized abortion, they are the poorest nations. They are afraid of the little one, they are afraid of the unborn child, and the child must die because they don't want to feed one more child, to educate one more child, the child must die."

The "nations who ha[d] legalized abortion" included the host country of the Nobel Peace Prize, which permitted abortion on demand, and the home countries of many of the distinguished guests in the audience. For more than a decade, laws removing protections for unborn children had been sweeping throughout both the Communist Bloc and Western societies. In Europe, Great Britain (1967), East Germany (1972), Denmark (1973), Hungary (1973), Bulgaria (1974), France (1975), Austria (1975), Sweden (1975), West Germany (1976), Yugoslavia (1977—1979), Norway (1978), Italy (1978), Luxembourg (1978), and Finland (1979) had recently passed laws weakening protections for babies in the womb. In the United States, Colorado became the first state to make abortion legal in 1967. Nineteen states followed in the next few years (with abortion remaining illegal in thirty states). In 1973, the United States Supreme Court took the decision away from the states, declaring abortion to be a constitutionally protected right in all fifty states.

To these, the "poorest" nations, Mother Teresa made a heartfelt plea: "And here I ask you, in the name of these little ones, for it was that unborn child that recognized the presence of Jesus when Mary came to visit Elizabeth, her cousin. As we read in the gospel, the moment Mary came into the house, the little one in the womb of his mother, leapt with joy, recognized the Prince of Peace. And so today, let us here make a strong resolution, we are going to save every little child, every unborn child, give them a chance to be born."

Mother Teresa's decision to use her platform on the world's stage—given to her as the recipient of the world's most prestigious prize—to criticize abortion supporters, was unexpected. Even for a Catholic nun. Because even Catholic nuns know that the world seeks affirmation, not truth. And yet, Mother Teresa chose not to affirm the world; neither did she choose the "safe" path of avoiding controversial topics. Rather, without regard for the loss of esteem of the "important" people praising her, she lovingly conveyed the message that she believed the world most needed to hear: at the hour of death, you are going to be judged not by the world's laws but by God's laws. She never indicated that she felt any fear in conveying this truth. The words of her favorite saint may reveal why. Saint Thérèse said, "Many people say, 'I don't have the courage to make this sacrifice.' Let them do what I did: exert a great effort. God never refuses that first grace which gives one the courage to act; afterwards the heart is strengthened."

Even the most ardent abortion supporters acknowledged the strength of Mother Teresa's heart.

Man's "Stupendous" Progress—and the Church's Unwavering Defense of God's Design

Mother Teresa was on solid theological ground when she asked the internationally televised Nobel Peace Prize audience to give every unborn child a chance to be born. Since the first century, the Catholic Church has affirmed the "unchangeable" teaching of the "moral evil of every procured abortion," warning that "formal cooperation in an abortion constitutes a grave offense."[417] The Church's teaching on abortion comes from the recognition of the "inviolable right of every innocent being to life,"[418] which must be "recognized and respected by civil society and the political authority."[419]

The immorality of abortion was uncontroversial until the 1960s, when a new wave of feminism spread throughout the Western world. In 1963, a book by Betty Friedan called

The Feminine Mystique was highly influential in animating "progressive" men and women to devalue motherhood and homemaking and believe that intelligent, sophisticated women had "more important" work to do than growing and strengthening families. The leaders of this movement taught women to understand their role in society through a lens of radical feminism: to see husbands not as partners but as oppressors, and children not as gifts from God but as impediments to worldly success. They sought to reshape society around their new ideology by creating groups advocating for "equality" and the legal recognition of "women's rights." Claiming that women would not be equal to men under the law until they had the "right" to engage in sexual activity without bearing a child, they advocated for governments to allow unfettered access to contraception and abortion. They achieved swift success in influencing nations. In just thirteen years, the United States government went from approving the use of the birth control pill (1960) to recognizing the use of contraception as a constitutionally protected right (1965) to legalizing abortion in most cases in twenty states (1967–72) to recognizing abortion as a constitutionally protected right (1973). In the same number of years, Britain's government went from allowing the federally funded health care system to prescribe the birth control pill (1961)[420] to legalizing abortion (1967) to offering free contraception to all women, regardless of marital status (1974).[421]

The Catholic Church, which is Christ's "instrument for the salvation of all,"[422] responded with clarity.

In 1968, Pope Paul VI published the encyclical *Humanae Vitae* ("Of Human Life"), condemning the use of contraception, sterilization, and abortion as "intrinsically wrong." In so doing, he marveled at "man's stupendous progress" in "endeavoring to extend his control over every aspect of his own life—over his body, over his mind and emotions, over his social life, and even over the laws that regulate the transmission of life"—in violation of God's design. He explained:

> An act of mutual love which impairs the capacity to transmit life which God the Creator, through specific laws, has built into it, frustrates His design which constitutes the norm of marriage, and contradicts the will of the Author of life. Hence to use this divine gift while depriving it, even if only partially, of its meaning and purpose, is equally repugnant to the nature of man and of woman, and is consequently in opposition to the plan of God and His holy will. But to experience the gift of married love while respecting the laws of conception is to acknowledge that one is not the master of the sources of life but rather the minister of the design established by the Creator. Just as man does not have unlimited dominion over his body in general, so also, and with more particular reason, he has no such dominion over his specifically sexual faculties, for these are concerned by their very nature with the generation of life, of which God is the source. "Human life is sacred—all men must recognize that fact," Our predecessor Pope John XXIII recalled. "From its very inception it reveals the creating hand of God."[423]

In 1974, the year after the United States Supreme Court

declared abortion to be a constitutionally protected right for all American women, Pope Paul VI ratified a *Declaration on Procured Abortion* by the Sacred Congregation for the Doctrine of the Faith. The Declaration noted that the Church's reason for not remaining silent on the topic of abortion was because she is "too conscious of the fact that it belongs to her vocation to defend man against everything that could disintegrate or lessen his dignity." The Declaration affirmed:

> Because the Son of God became man, there is no man who is not His brother in humanity and who is not called to become a Christian in order to receive salvation from Him.
>
> The commandment of God is formal: "You shall not kill" (Ex. 20:13). Life is at the same time a gift and a responsibility. It is received as a "talent" (cf. Mt. 25:14–30); it must be put to proper use. In order that life may bring forth fruit, many tasks are offered to man in this world and he must not shirk them. More important still, the Christian knows that eternal life depends on what, with the grace of God, he does with his life on earth. . . . Divine law and natural reason, therefore, exclude all right to the direct killing of an innocent man. . . . All publicly recognized freedom is always limited by the certain rights of others.

Thus, the Church proclaimed, the "first right of the human person is his life." It is "the condition of all the others." Hence it "must be protected above all others."[424]

A Fearless Defender of Life

Mother Teresa's ministry to the poorest of the poor included many of the most powerful and influential figures in the world who championed the "right" to kill babies in the womb. Her love for Christ, who had been a "little one in the womb of His mother," cultivated in her heart a burning desire to imitate His perfect love for all humanity. Jesus was a teacher who courageously shared hard truths. Throughout His public ministry, He brought "good news to the poor . . . and recover[y] of sight to the blind" (Lk 4:18), but He did not convert all sinners. So, too, Mother Teresa shared the good news of Jesus's saving love with the poor and blind people of the world; among the poorest and blindest were the supporters of abortion.

As the world tightened its embrace of what Pope John Paul II would call "the culture of death,"[425] Mother Teresa made her pro-life advocacy a defining part of the final decades of her ministry. In 1980, at the request of Pope John Paul II, she participated in the World Synod of Bishops in Rome, where she urged priests to be holier spiritual leaders for families; the synod concluded by reaffirming the Church's teaching on abortion and contraception.[426] That same year, she joined demonstrations in Italy by the Movement for Life.[427] In 1981, she addressed pro-life congressmen and senators at a symposium hosted by the American Family Institute in Washington, DC. Later that year, she took the opportunity of being awarded an honorary doctorate of medicine from Rome's Catholic University to condemn the medical practice of intentionally killing babies in the womb, saying from the podium, "Abortion is nothing but the fear of the child—fear to have to feed one more child, to have to educate one more child, to have to love one more child. Therefore the child must die."[428]

In 1982, she attended a pro-life convention in St. Louis, a pro-life rally in Glasgow, and a news conference in Dublin organized by the Society for the Protection of the Unborn Child.[429] In 1993, she met with pro-life campaigners in Dublin, pleading with the crowd, "Let us make one strong resolution that in this beautiful country of Ireland no child may be unwanted. . . . Let us promise Our Lady who loves Ireland so much that we will never have in this country one single abortion."[430]

In addition to appearing at public events, Mother Teresa granted many interviews with broadcast and print journalists who delivered her message throughout the world. She often used these occasions to speak out about the evil of abortion. As her authorized biographer, Kathryn Spink, related, she took "every opportunity to speak out in defense of the unborn child, no matter how controversial her views might be."[431]

In 1989, American journalist William F. Buckley Jr. interviewed Mother Teresa on his popular television show, *Firing Line*. While discussing her humanitarian work, he asked if God enjoins His people to try "to make a better world." She answered, "Yes," people are "bound in conscience to do everything possible" to help others. And then, without being asked about the controversial topic, she offered a hard truth that she knew would offend Americans who considered the "right" to abortion to be sacrosanct. "Concern for others needs to begin before conception," she said, explaining, "They have to decide before conception, not after conception. That child has a right to live. Just as you or I. That little one, that little unborn child has a right to live. It has been created for greater things, to love and to be loved. It has full rights just like anybody."

Mother Teresa's passionately pro-life values made her the target of vicious attacks by abortion activists. In 1990, celebrated feminist Germaine Greer attempted to discredit her by accusing her of mistreating rape victims nearly twenty years earlier in Dhaka, Bangladesh. In an article published in *Independent Magazine* about pregnant women in Dhaka who "needed" abortions, she wrote, "Mother Teresa offered them no option but to bear the offspring of hate. There is no room in Mother Teresa's universe for the moral priorities of others. There is no question of offering suffering women a choice. Secular aid workers told me at the time that women with complications of late pregnancy, caused by physical abuse and malnutrition, as well as women miscarrying, were turning up at clinics claiming to have been accused of attempted abortion and turned away by Mother Teresa's nuns."[432]

Unfounded criticism by Greer and other abortion apologists had little to no effect. It neither stopped Mother Teresa from exposing the evil of abortion nor sullied her reputation as a selfless humanitarian. In deference to truth, she never diluted her message to avoid confrontation and conflict, even in the company of powerful abortion supporters. And yet, she remained nearly universally admired for her goodness, even among many of the most passionate opponents of the right to life.

This explains why, on February 3, 1994, Mother Teresa once again found herself at a major event with pro-abortion world leaders. United States president Bill Clinton had invited her to give the keynote address at the annual National Prayer Breakfast in Washington, DC. President Clinton and his wife, First Lady Hillary Clinton, were known to be staunch abortion supporters. One of President Clinton's first acts in office was expediting the drug approval process for the controversial abortion pill RU-486. Another was appointing Hillary to lead a task force on National Health Reform—an initiative through which Hillary sought to make abortion "widely available" through an overhaul of the country's health care system.[433]

Nearly three thousand people attended the prayer breakfast, including liberals and conservatives, Democrats and Republicans, Christians, Jews, Muslims, agnostics, and atheists.[434] Distinguished guests included President Clinton and the first lady, Vice President Al Gore and his wife, Tipper Gore, along with Supreme Court justices and members of Congress.

Mother Teresa spoke straightforwardly about Jesus, salvation, damnation, sin, sacrifice, and the obligation to love our neighbor. She said:

> It is not enough for us to say: "I love God," but I also have to love my neighbor. St. John says that you are a liar if you say you love God and you don't love your neighbor. How can you love God whom you do not

see, if you do not love your neighbor whom you see, whom you touch, with whom you live? And so it is very important for us to realize that love, to be true, has to hurt. I must be willing to give whatever it takes not to harm other people and, in fact, to do good to them. This requires that I be willing to give until it hurts. Otherwise, there is not true love in me and I bring injustice, not peace, to those around me.

Thirteen minutes into her speech, she made the same bold declaration she had made to the Nobel Peace Prize audience fifteen years earlier: "But I feel that the greatest destroyer of peace today is abortion, because Jesus said, 'If you receive a little child, you receive me.' So every abortion is the denial of receiving Jesus, the neglect of receiving Jesus."

Peggy Noonan, a former speechwriter for President Ronald Reagan who was at the prayer breakfast, reported a "cool deep silence" from the audience that lasted 1.3 seconds, followed by applause that lasted five or six minutes.[435]

But not everyone applauded. Some audience members sat as still as statues; one took out a notepad and wrote out a to-do list.[436] Most conspicuously, President Clinton, Hillary Clinton, Vice President Al Gore, and Tipper Gore, did not clap. As Paul Kengor noted, "They sat there, in the glare of the hot lights, all eyes in the crowd fixed upon them, as they tried not to move or be noticed, conspicuous in their lack of response, clearly uncomfortable as the applause raged on."[437]

When the applause finally stopped, Mother Teresa picked up where she left off, calling abortion a "war against the child" and "murder by the mother herself." She spoke about the rights of the innocent child and the harm that spreads throughout the world as a result of violence perpetrated against babies in the womb. All in all, Mother Teresa spent more than nine minutes of her thirty-four-minute speech pleading with her distinguished audience to recognize the humanity of unborn children in accordance with God's law.

Hillary Clinton wrote in her memoir that, following her remarks, Mother Teresa spoke to her privately: "[She] was unerringly direct. She disagreed with my views on a woman's right to choose and told me so."[438]

Inheriting the Kingdom Prepared for Her

The Gospel of Matthew records Jesus saying to His disciples:

> When the Son of man comes in his glory, and all the angels with him, then he will sit on his glorious throne. Before him will be gathered all the nations, and he will separate them one from another as a shepherd separates the sheep from the goats, and he will place the sheep at his right hand, but the goats at the left. Then the King will say to those at his right hand, "Come, O blessed of my Father, inherit the kingdom prepared for you from the foundation of the world; for I was hungry and you gave me food, I was thirsty and you gave me drink, I was a stranger and you welcomed me, I was naked and you clothed me, I was sick and you visited me, I was in prison and you came to me." Then the righteous will answer him, "Lord, when did we see thee hungry and feed thee, or thirsty and give

thee drink? And when did we see thee a stranger and welcome thee, or naked and clothe thee? And when did we see thee sick or in prison and visit thee?" And the King will answer them, "Truly, I say to you, as you did it to one of the least of these my brethren, you did it to me." (Mt 25:31–40)

Mother Teresa died on September 9, 1997, after a lifetime of loving the "least" of Jesus's brothers. Through her selfless love, she imitated His perfect love. And through His saving grace, she "inherit[ed] the Kingdom prepared for [her] from the foundation of the world."

On World Mission Sunday, October 19, 2003, Pope John Paul II beatified Mother Teresa, calling her a "diminutive woman in love with God, a humble Gospel messenger, and a tireless benefactor of humanity."[439] Thirteen years later, on September 4, 2016, Pope Francis officially declared her a saint. At her canonization Mass, he noted her "defense of human life, those unborn and those abandoned and discarded," and he praised her for "ceaselessly proclaiming" that "the unborn are the weakest, the smallest, the most vulnerable."[440]

Mother Teresa—now known as Saint Teresa of Calcutta—once said, "I am a little pencil in the hand of a writing God who is sending a love letter to the world." The sentiment is at the same time playful and deeply meaningful; it is reminiscent of Saint Thérèse of Lisieux's "way of spiritual childhood" through which Thérèse imagined herself to be a "little brush" painting His Likeness on souls.[441]

Through full surrender to God's will, Mother Teresa

showed extraordinary courage in condemning evil in the presence of powerful apologists for evil. The source of her courage was simple: love. The First Letter of John explains: "There is no fear in love, but perfect love casts out fear. For fear has to do with punishment, and he who fears is not perfected in love" (1 Jn 4:18).

Saint Teresa of Calcutta, pray for us.

Conclusion

The world has been a dangerous place for God's people since the beginning of time. But it has been an even more dangerous place for His enemies. It is fitting that this book begins with Saint Joan of Arc—because her story cannot be told without harkening back to the first great battle between good and evil.

In the beginning, God made all the angels for a singular purpose: to love and serve Him for eternity. The angel Michael embraced his purpose out of a sense of justice and gratitude; he owed his existence to God and would use his free will to do His will. But the angel Lucifer rejected the very purpose of his being; overcome with pride and envy, he would abuse his freedom to pursue his own will.

Lucifer imagined an alternative world order with him, not Christ, at the head. He lacked God's power to create beings out of nothing, so he was resigned to preying on God's creatures, using his intelligence to distract and dissuade them from fulfilling their true purpose. He persuaded other angels to join him. They could not remain in heaven because they were not good and pure, so the great battle between good and evil broke out, with Michael commanding the angels loyal to God and Lucifer commanding the angels loyal to their evil desires. Michael's army won and God cast the bad angels out of heaven forever.

There is no greater punishment for any of God's creatures than to lose the "supreme, definitive happiness" of being in eternal communion with the Most Holy Trinity, the Blessed Mother, and the angels and saints in heaven. Locked out of heaven, Satan "enjoys" a certain dominion over the world that will end at Jesus's second coming—but it is a hopeless, joyless, pathetic existence. As he and his minions "prowl about the world seeking the ruin of souls," his power is limited by what God allows in accordance with His saving plan. Most significantly, he is powerless to interfere with the outpouring of grace that flows from God to humans, assisting us to respond to His call to participate in His divine life.[442]

The *Catechism of the Catholic Church* tells us that "those who die in God's grace and friendship and are perfectly purified live with God for ever with Christ."[443] And "they are like God for ever, for they 'see Him as He is,' face to face" in heaven.

God exists outside of time. His plan for the world has always included the creation of every human who has ever existed and ever will exist. God's timing is perfect, as is His knowledge of the past, present, and future. He wills all humans to come into the world at a precise time and place to fulfill a specific purpose—and He has a unique path to heaven for each of us. He knows and uses for our sanctification the families we are born into, the people we will encounter, and the events and culture of the world that shape our lives.

God has a plan, and it is perfect as He is perfect, but it is perfect on His terms—not our terms. God's plan is rooted in love and freedom, not coercion. He does not force anyone to reciprocate His love; such an act would defy the reality of the meaning and purpose of love. Rather, He confers on humans the power to know and love Him. He pursues us in a myriad of ways. His plan is for us to respond to His call, freely; it requires our participation.

As the story of the first great battle between good and evil illustrates, God's creatures can reject His saving plan by choosing their will over His will—with eternal consequences. The book of Revelation warns:

> I heard a great voice from the throne saying, "Behold, the dwelling of God is with men. He will dwell with them, and they shall be his people, and God himself will be with them; he will wipe away every tear from their eyes, and death shall be no more, neither shall there be mourning nor crying nor pain any more, for the former things have passed away."
>
> And he who sat upon the throne said, "Behold, I make all things new." Also he said, "Write this, for these words are trustworthy and true." And he said to me, "It is done! I am the Alpha and the Omega, the beginning and the end. To the thirsty I will give water without price from the fountain of the water of life. He who conquers shall have this heritage, and I will be his God and he shall be my son. But as for the

cowardly, the faithless, the polluted, as for murderers, fornicators, sorcerers, idolaters, and all liars, their lot shall be in the lake that burns with fire and brimstone, which is the second death."(Rv 21:3–8)

It is worth noting that the first group of people identified as not inheriting eternal life are "cowards." Cowardice, of course, is a lack of courage. C. S. Lewis defined courage as "not just one of the virtues but the form of every virtue at the testing point."[444]

It is not just cowardice, but also "lukewarm" works that threaten the eternal life of souls. See this warning, also in the book of Revelation: "I know your works: you are neither cold nor hot. Would that you were cold or hot! So, because you are lukewarm, and neither cold nor hot, I will spew you out of my mouth" (Rv 3:15–16).

We live in a post-Christian society that celebrates sin as virtue, rejects the existence of objective truth—especially the truth that Jesus Christ is "the way, the truth, and the life"—and punishes nonconformists as "haters" through shaming, slander, ostracization, and "canceling." Christians who are immersed in the world, without appreciating the soul-sacrificing dangers of the world, will have great difficulty being courageous "at the testing point."

No one knows how many souls will be admitted to the glory of heaven. The Catholic Church is silent on the matter, except in her canonization of more than ten thousand saints. Jesus, however, warned that "few" would be saved. The Gospel of Matthew records Him saying, "Enter by the narrow gate; for the gate is wide and the way is easy, that leads to

CONCLUSION   193

destruction, and those who enter by it are many. For the gate is narrow and the way is hard, that leads to life, and those who find it are few" (Mt 7:13–14). Similarly, when Jesus was asked if only a few people would be saved, He answered, "Strive to enter by the narrow door; for many, I tell you, will seek to enter and will not be able" (Lk 13:24).

The fourteen saints in this book are among those who were "strong enough" to enter through the narrow door of salvation. God had a plan for each of them that began before He "formed them in the womb" (see Jer 1:5). The plan included not only the circumstances of the saints' lives but the events of the world that happened up to that point, including the heroic examples of the saints whose stories occupied a special place in their imaginations.

- Joan of Arc grew up hearing the stories of Saint Michael the Archangel, Saint Margaret of Antioch, and Saint Catherine of Alexandria. Devotion to all three saints was strong in medieval France. Saint Michael was the patron of the French royal family and soldiers fighting against faithless armies. Many French sites were named after Saint Michael, including at least forty-six churches in Joan's neighboring dioceses. Joan's village had a special devotion to Saint Margaret. There was a statue of Saint Margaret in Joan's parish church. Saint Catherine's feast day was a holy day of obligation. Nearly all churches at the time had a statue of her in them and many

churches were named after her, including a
church near Joan's village.

- Jose Luis Sánchez del Rio grew up with a
strong devotion to Our Lady of Guadalupe, who promised to be a "compassionate
mother" to the people of Mexico. He grew up
hearing about Saint Juan Diego's encounter
with Our Lady that converted virtually all of
Mexico to Catholicism. He heard the stories
of Anacleto González Flores and Saint Tarcisius at critical times during his short life. It
was soon after visiting Flores's grave that he
made the decision to enlist in the Cristeros
army. At camp, the older Christeros soldiers
affectionately called him "Tarcisius" after the
twelve-year-old early Christian martyr who
had a deep love for Christ, really present, in
the Blessed Sacrament.

- Jerzy Popiełuszko loved learning about the
lives of the saints when he was a boy. His
favorite saint was Maximilian Kolbe. He used
to read *Knights of the Immaculata,* the Catholic
newspaper founded by Father Maximilian, at
his grandmother's house. When he attended
a secondary boarding school, his favorite
works were books about Maximilian Kolbe
and a collection of sermons by Cardinal Stefan Wyszyński. He attended a seminary led by
Cardinal Wyszyński, who ordained him. He
was sitting in one of the front rows when Pope

John Paul II visited Poland on June 2, 1979, hearing the Polish pope say, "I cry—I who am a son of the land of Poland and who am also Pope John Paul II—I cry from all the depths of this Millennium, I cry on the vigil of Pentecost. Let your Spirit descend. Let your Spirit descend. And renew the face of the earth, the face of this land."

- Agnes Gonxha Bojaxhiu was born thirteen years after the death of Saint Thérèse of Lisieux. When she was a young girl, devotion to Saint Thérèse's spread throughout the world as the young saint's autobiography, *Story of a Soul*, became one of the most-read books of all time. When Agnes joined the Loreto Order and had to choose a name, she chose "Sister Mary Teresa of the Child Jesus" in honor of Saint Thérèse of Lisieux.

Born at different times in different parts of the world, the heroes in this book shared an extraordinary love for Christ, gratitude for His sacrifice on the cross, and humility in knowing that everything they possessed—their talents, their achievements, even their lives—came from God, belonged to Him, and must be used to glorify Him. They were raised in faithfully Catholic families. As children, they received the sacraments of Christian initiation, attended Mass regularly, received grace from the sacraments, prayed the Rosary, and witnessed charity in their homes. They also practiced acts of virtue on a regular basis.

Catholic parents have a duty to provide a Catholic education to their children that includes proper catechesis and an immersion in the intellectual and sacramental traditions of the Church. Knowledge of the stories of the saints—the men, women, and children who have navigated the challenges of the world to emerge victorious in friendship with Christ in heaven—is an essential part of this education. In addition, it is critical that parents model moral courage; children must see their parents refusing to compromise on truth. They must make it clear that "getting ahead" in the world and "getting along" with the world are not worth sacrificing one's soul.

Jesus knew that His followers would be tempted to conform to the sinfulness of the world in a misguided pursuit of peace. That's why He told His disciples:

> Do not think that I have come to bring peace on earth; I have not come to bring peace, but a sword. For I have come to set a man against his father, and a daughter against her mother, and a daughter-in-law against her mother-in-law; and a man's foes will be those of his own household. He who loves father or mother more than me is not worthy of me; and he who loves son or daughter more than me is not worthy of me; and he who does not take his cross and follow me is not worthy of me. He who finds his life will lose it, and he who loses his life for my sake will find it. (Mt 10:34–39)

The saints in this book found eternal life because they loved Christ more than their own lives. Beginning at a young age, they sought to unite their will with God's will. As a result, they practiced acts of courage and developed a habit of courageously choosing Christ over their own comfort. By the time they encountered their greatest "testing points," they were able to endure almost unimaginable pain, suffering, and temptation.

- During the final months of Joan of Arc's life following her capture by the English, she refused to affirm the lies of her indictment and conviction, instead choosing truth and death by burning at the stake. Three years of courageous acts, beginning with her leaving home at the age of sixteen to make the outrageous request of commanding an army, helped her develop a habit of courage.

- During the final nine days of José Luis Sánchez del Rio's life following his capture by the Federales, he refused to renounce his Catholic faith, instead choosing torture and an agonizing death witnessed by his family. Three years of courageous acts, beginning with him providing illegal religious instruction to the children in town, even taking them to visit Jesus in the Blessed Sacrament, helped him develop a habit of courage.

- During the last two and half years of Jerzy Popiełuszko's life, he continued to preach about the truth of the Faith and the illegitimacy of the communist government,

enduring increasing harassment and intimidation from the communists that resulted in
his brutal murder. A lifetime of courageous
acts, beginning with his service as an altar boy
at daily Mass, despite warnings from his communist school, helped him develop a habit of
courage.

• At the end of a decade in which laws removing protections for unborn children had
been sweeping throughout the West, Mother
Teresa used her platform as the recipient of
the Nobel Peace Prize to condemn abortion
as "the greatest destroyer of peace today" and
the nations that had legalized abortion as "the
poorest nations." A lifetime of courageous
acts, especially since pursuing a new order
serving "the poorest of the poor" thirty-three
years earlier, helped her develop a habit of
courage.

All Catholics can imitate the saints in this book by practicing courage for Christ in everyday moments. Here are ten
practical ideas to help anyone—most importantly parents
modeling behavior for children and young adults making
their own decisions in the world—develop a habit of moral
courage:

1. Wear a crucifix, miraculous medal, scapular,
   religious t-shirt, or other religious item.
2. Display religious items inside and outside a
   home, dorm room, or office.

3. Find opportunities to talk about going to Mass, confession, or adoration, particularly when asked, "What did you do [yesterday, over the weekend, etc.]?"

4. "Like" a friend's post about Christianity or the truth of the Faith on social media, especially regarding a controversial truth that runs counter to woke culture.

5. Post a Christian message on social media (for example, posting pictures from the March for Life).

6. Pray before meals in public.

7. Decline a "pride" flag (at work, school, on social media, etc.) that celebrates sinful behavior that is offensive to God.

8. Refuse to participate in any activity celebrating sinful behavior.

9. Challenge modern ideas and assumptions when Christian beliefs are ridiculed or dismissed in casual conversation or in a more formal setting, including work or class.

10. Offer public support to other Christians who stand up for Christian beliefs in a group setting.

But the single best way to imitate the saints is by discerning God's will and making it the driving force in our lives. We must be like the blind man in the Gospel of Luke:

> As he drew near to Jericho, a blind man was sitting by the roadside begging; and hearing a multitude going

by, he inquired what this meant. They told him, "Jesus of Nazareth is passing by." And he cried, "Jesus, Son of David, have mercy on me!" And those who were in front rebuked him, telling him to be silent; but he cried out all the more, "Son of David, have mercy on me!" And Jesus stopped, and commanded him to be brought to him; and when he came near, he asked him, "What do you want me to do for you?" He said, "Lord, let me receive my sight." And Jesus said to him, "Receive your sight; your faith has made you well." And immediately he received his sight and followed him, glorifying God; and all the people, when they saw it, gave praise to God. (Lk 18:35–43)

The final lesson of this book is this: all Christians must tell Jesus we want to "see." The best place to do this is in front of the Blessed Sacrament, the Body, Blood, Soul, and Divinity of Jesus Christ. Once Christ gives us sight—when we are able to discern His will for our lives—we must follow Him wherever he leads. Others will see the lived reality of our faith—continuing the great witness of evangelization that is exemplified in the lives of the saints—and they, too, will give praise to God.

And heaven will be our reward.

Notes

1   *CCC* 2222–28.

2   Chesterton, *The Catholic Church and Conversion*, 30.

3   Stearns, "Happy Children: A Modern Emotional Commitment."

4   John Paul II, "Address by the Holy Father John Paul II," no. 2.

5   "So far as the facts of [Joan's] life are concerned, it is astonishing to learn that we have more detailed evidence about her than anyone else in the history of the world up to her time. We know far more about Joan, for example, than we do about Moses, Plato, Jesus of Nazareth, Alexander the Great, Julius Caesar, Buddha or Muhammed. For the last two and a half years of her life, we can construct almost a day-by-day account of her whereabouts and actions. We also have several letters she dictated, three of them bearing her simple signature." Spoto, *Joan*, xi.

6   This often-quoted statement from Joan comes from the testimony of Henri Le Royer, her host in Vaucouleurs, who recalled a conversation with Joan about the danger of the English soldiers who were "everywhere" on the road she would travel to Chinon to meet the king. Henri testified, "When she sought to go, she was asked how she would do it, when there were so many men-at-arms everywhere. She answered that she feared not men-at-arms for her way was open, and if there were men-at-arms on her road, she had God, her Lord, who would clear the way for her to go to the lord Dauphin, and that she had been born to do this." Spoto, 36.

7　Spoto, 28.

8　Pernoud, *Joan of Arc*, 16.

9　Spoto, *Joan*, 3.

10　Pernoud, *Joan of Arc,* 16.

11　Pernoud, 16–20.

12　Pernoud, 16–20.

13　"Ever since the Norman conquest of England there had been three great powers in Europe: the German and Italian domains of the Holy Roman Empire; France; and England." Carroll, *The Glory of Christendom*, 381.

14　Carroll, 383.

15　Carroll, 514.

16　Carroll, 514.

17　Carroll, 514.

18　Carroll, 514.

19　Carroll, 515.

20　Carroll, 515.

21　Carroll, 516.

22　Pernoud, *Joan of Arc,* 30.

23　Pernoud, 30.

24　See Luke 1:37.

25　"Quis Ut Deus, Who's Like God."

26　*CCC* 1731, 1733.

27　*CCC* 1733.

28　Marison, *A Popular Abridgement of The Mystical City of God*, 19–20. Venerable Mother Mary of Jesus of Agreda (1602–65) was a Spanish nun whose 2,676-page history of the creation of the world is based on revelations given to her by the Blessed Virgin Mary. She was declared venerable by Pope Clement X. Her body is incorrupt and on display in the Church of the Conceptionists Convent in Ágreda, Spain.

29　Marison, 19–20.

30　Marison, 21.

31　Marison, 22.

32   Marison, 22.

33   Marison, 22.

34   Marison, 22.

35   Marison, 23.

36   Jude 1:9.

37   Daniel 12:1.

38   Daniel 10:13.

39   Daniel 10:21.

40   Revelation 12:7.

41   See Benedictine Convent, *St. Michael the Archangel*, 8–9, which states, "The Fathers of the Church tell us that even though in many instances the name of St. Michael is not mentioned in Holy Scripture, when reference is made to the services of an angel, we may confidently believe that it was either St. Michael himself who rendered assistance, or his angelic subjects, who did so at his command."

42   Benedictine Convent, *St. Michael the Archangel*, 11–12.

43   "Constantine the Great."

44   In medieval France, the flag of the king bore Saint Michael's image. Soldiers routinely invoked his protection and intercession with prayerful songs on the battlefield. Spoto, *Joan*, 17–18.

45   "That [Margaret] existed and was martyred are probably true; all else is probably fictitious embroidery added to her story, which was immensely popular in the Middle Ages, spreading from the East all over Western Europe." Delaney, *Dictionary of Saints*, 380–81.

46   Eusebius, the scholar and Bishop of Caesarea who wrote extensively about the events of the developing Church, recorded that people flocked to Christianity. "Diocletian."

47   "Diocletian."

48   "Diocletian."

49   Delaney, *Dictionary of Saints*, 381.

50   Delaney, 381.

51   Delaney, 381.

52 Delaney, 381.

53 "Alexandria."

54 The Dioclesian persecution began in 303 and lasted for seven years after his abdication in 305. "Diocletian."

55 Carroll, *The Founding of Christendom*, 506–7.

56 Carroll, 526.

57 Kosloski, "The 18-year-old who defied an emperor."

58 Delaney, *Dictionary of Saints*, 138.

59 "Saint Catherine of Alexandria."

60 Spoto, *Joan*, 19.

61 Spoto, 29.

62 Pernoud, *Joan of Arc*, 23–24.

63 Pernoud, 23.

64 Spoto, *Joan*, 29.

65 Spoto, 34.

66 Pernoud, *Joan of Arc*, 21; Spoto, *Joan*, 34.

67 Spoto, *Joan*, 34.

68 Spoto, 35.

69 Pernoud, *Joan of Arc*, 32.

70 Pernoud, 36.

71 Pernoud, 37.

72 Spoto, *Joan*, 36.

73 "The Battle of the Herrings."

74 Spoto, *Joan*, 35.

75 Spoto, 35.

76 Spoto, 35.

77 Spoto, 36.

78 Pernoud, *Joan of Arc*, 39.

79 Pernoud, 40.

80 Pernoud, 41; Spoto, *Joan*, 39–40.

81 Spoto, *Joan*, 40.

82 Spoto, 40.

83 Spoto, 40.

84 Spoto, 42.

85   Spoto, 43.

86   Spoto, 43.

87   Spoto, 47.

88   Spoto, 48.

89   "When I entered my King's room, I knew him among the others by the counsel of my voice which revealed him to me. I told my King that I wanted. . . . The voice had promised me that, as soon as I came to the King, he himself would receive me." Pernoud, *Joan of Arc,* 46.

90   Quoting Raoul de Gaucourt, a chamberlain, knight, and governor of Orléans. Spoto, *Joan,* 48. Also, "almost all contemporary writers remarked on Charles's agreeable, even handsome, appearance." Spoto, 46.

91   Quoting Jean Pasquerel, a hermit of Saint-Augustin and subsequently Joan's confessor. Pernoud, *Joan of Arc,* 52–53.

92   Carroll notes that the secret probably involved "specific elements of a prayer that he had offered that God would assure him of his own legitimacy (which he and others doubted because of his father's madness and his mother's reputed promiscuity); that he alone rather than his whole country should be punished if the troubles which had come upon France were due in any way to his sins; and that God would forgive the French people if it was their sins which had angered Him." Carroll, *The Glory of Christendom,* 518.

93   Pernoud, *Joan of Arc,* 49.

94   "Jean Duke of Alençon."

95   "Jean Duke of Alençon."

96   Spoto, *Joan,* 50.

97   Spoto, 50.

98   Spoto, 50; Pernoud, *Joan of Arc,* 54.

99   Spoto, *Joan,* 53.

100   Pernoud, *Joan of Arc,* 58.

101   Pernoud, 70–71.

102   "Her Battle Standard."

[103] "Her Battle Standard."

[104] Spoto, *Joan*, 63–64.

[105] "Siege of Orléans."

[106] "Siege of Orléans."

[107] "Siege of Orléans."

[108] Pernoud, *Joan of Arc*, 81.

[109] "Siege of Orléans."

[110] Pernoud, *Joan of Arc*, 82.

[111] Pernoud, 83–84.

[112] Pernoud, 83.

[113] Carroll, *The Glory of Christendom*, 520.

[114] Carroll, 87.

[115] Pernoud, *Joan of Arc*, 87.

[116] "Jean Duke of Alençon."

[117] Pernoud, *Joan of Arc*, 93.

[118] Pernoud, 90.

[119] Pernoud, 90.

[120] "Her Battle Standard."

[121] Spoto, *Joan*, 105.

[122] Spoto, 101.

[123] Spoto, 105.

[124] Spoto, 110–12.

[125] Spoto, 112.

[126] Spoto, 112.

[127] Spoto, 118.

[128] Spoto, 123.

[129] "Joan's Leap for Freedom."

[130] Spoto, *Joan*, 127.

[131] Spoto, 135.

[132] Spoto, 132.

[133] Spoto, 133.

[134] Spoto, 141.

[135] Spoto, 141.

[136] Spoto, 137.

137 The Old Testament prohibition against cross-dressing was intended to protect the Israelites from worshipping pagan gods, including the Mesopotamian goddess, Ishtar, whose followers engaged in orgies, transvestism, and other sexual sin. Christian theologians had interpreted much of the guidance appearing before and after the cross-dressing prohibition in the same chapter of Deuteronomy—including directives to punish adulterers and prostitutes by death and prohibitions against wearing "cloth made from wool and linen woven together"—as applying narrowly to ancient times. Spoto, 142–44.

138 Spoto, 143.
139 Spoto, 144.
140 Spoto, 165.
141 Spoto, 167.
142 Spoto, 174–75.
143 Spoto, 179.
144 Spoto, 180–81.
145 Spoto, 182.
146 Pernoud, *Joan of Arc*, 229.
147 Pernoud, 188.
148 Cerrone, *For God and Country*, 144.
149 Pernoud, *Joan of Arc*, 230–31.
150 Spoto, *Joan*, 189.
151 Spoto, 189.
152 Cerrone, *For God and Country*, 146.
153 Jesus Christ taught that married people "are no longer two but one" (Mt 19:6).
154 Spoto, *Joan*, 150.
155 Elarde, "Our Lady of Guadalupe."
156 "José Anacleto González Flores and eight Companions."
157 "St. Juan Diego."
158 Chavez, *Our Lady of Guadalupe and Saint Juan Diego*, xxvii.
159 Carroll, *The Cleaving of Christendom*, 22.
160 Carroll, 22.

[161]   Kerkhove, "Dark Religion?" Kerkhove writes that the Aztects considered sacrificial death to be a "glorious end." He notes that Fr. Diego Duran, a Dominican missionary in New Spain in the sixteenth century, wrote that Aztecs ridiculed the "weakness of the Christians" and applauded "the sacrifice of human beings . . . [as] the honoured oblation of great lords and noblemen. They remember these things and tell of them as if they had been great deeds."

[162]   Kerkhove, 142.

[163]   Kerkhove, 142.

[164]   Carlson, "Abortion."

[165]   The Aztecs believed that the god Tlaloc would not accept a child sacrifice unless the child cried. Carlson, "Abortion."

[166]   Kerkhove, "Dark Religion?," 140.

[167]   Carroll, *The Cleaving of Christendom,* 30.

[168]   "Catholic Church and the Age of Discovery."

[169]   Chavez, *Our Lady of Guadalupe and Saint Juan Diego,* 4.

[170]   Friar Geronimo de Mendieta reported the mistreatment of the natives by the Spaniards in his book *Historia Eclesiastica Indiana*: "As the Spaniards at that time saw themselves as lords of such an extensive land, populated by countless people, and all of them subdued and obedient to whatever the Spaniards wished to order, the Spaniards lived abusively, each one as he wished and fancied, exercising all types of vices. They treated the Indigenous with such harshness and cruelty that paper and time would not suffice to tell all the humiliations which they did to them in particular. Not being able to keep up with the Spaniards, they would sell the land they owned to usurer merchants. . . . They sold the children of the poor, who became slaves. . . . The Friars, seeing how inconvenient it was for the Indigenous to have to go through those humiliations and then to love our faith and Christian religion, would preach against those vices and sins which were committed in public, and would rebuke them publicly and personally with full Christian liberty. When those who governed [that also participated in these crimes and other worse ones, such as to enslave people as they

wished] saw this, they turned agaist the Friars as if they were terrible enemies." Chavez, *Our Lady of Guadalupe and Saint Juan Diego*, 7.

[171] Chavez, 8.

[172] Chavez, xxx.

[173] Chavez, 9.

[174] Chavez, 9.

[175] Chavez, 10.

[176] Chavez, 10.

[177] Chavez, 15.

[178] Elarde, "Our Lady of Guadalupe."

[179] Carroll, *The Cleaving of Christendom*, 30.

[180] Murphy, *Saints and Sinners in the Cristero War*, 20.

[181] The Vatican delegated authority to the crown to nominate bishops, control the number of priests coming from Europe to the New World, earn considerable revenue through taxation of the Church, and even veto the publication and execution of papal edicts in the colonies. See Murphy, 25.

[182] The Catholic Church was the only institution in the colony providing services for the poor through hospitals, schools, and orphanages. Murphy, 24.

[183] Murphy, 26.

[184] Murphy, 31.

[185] His birthday is a national holiday in Mexico.

[186] Murphy, *Saints and Sinners in the Cristero War*, 36–37.

[187] Dominic, "Saint Miguel Pro, A Modern Martyr."

[188] Medina, "When the Marxists Tried to Take Over Mexico."

[189] Medina, "When the Marxists Tried to Take Over Mexico."

[190] "Relación Política México – Rusia."

[191] Jasper, "Movie on Cristeros War Exposes Mexican Govt.'s Anti-Christian Campaign."

[192] Ferreira, *Blessed José Luis Sánchez del Río*, 6.

[193] Encyclopedia.com, s.v. "Mora Y Del Rio, José (1854-1928)."

[194] Villa, "St. José Sánchez del Río."

[195] "Claims about the Tilma and the Image."

[196] Villa, "St. José Sánchez del Río."

[197] Villa, "St. José Sánchez del Río."

[198] *CCC* 1285.

[199] Fr. Enrique Amezcua founded the Priestly Confraternity of the Labourers of the Kingdom of Christ, and Fr. Marcial Maciel founded the Legionaries of Christ. Ferreira, *Blessed José Luis Sánchez del Río*, 10.

[200] *CCC* 791.

[201] Pope Pius XI, *Iniquis Afflictisque*, November 18, 1926, https://www.vatican.va/content/pius-xi/en/encyclicals/documents/hf_p-xi_enc_18111926_iniquis-afflictisque.html.

[202] "The Cristero War."

[203] The Nicene Creed is the profession of faith of Catholics.

[204] "Blessed Anacleto González Flores."

[205] Murphy, *Saints and Sinners in the Cristero War*, 54–55.

[206] Breslin, "Catholic Heroes . . . Blessed Anacelto Gonzales Flores."

[207] Murphy, *Saints and Sinners in the Cristero War*, 55.

[208] Murphy, 55–56.

[209] Murphy, 48.

[210] Murphy, 57.

[211] Peterson, "Famous last words."

[212] Murphy, *Saints and Sinners in the Cristero War*, 70.

[213] Murphy, 154.

[214] Anacleto was quoting the Ecuadoran President Gabriel Garcia Moreno, who had been assassinated for his defense of the Catholic faith in 1875. "Bl. Analceto González Flores: Spiritual Leader of the Cristeros."

[215] This was one witness's account. Hoffman, "The true story of For Greater Glory."

[216] Hoffman.

[217] "Apostolic letter by which the Supreme Pontiff Benedict XVI has raised to the glory of the altars the servants of God."

[218] "José Anacleto González Flores and eight Companions."

219 Rubio, "Saint José Luis Sánchez del Río."

220 Check, "Viva Cristo Rey!"

221 Check, "Viva Cristo Rey!"

222 Rubio, "Saint José Luis Sánchez del Río."

223 Pope Damasus had an inscription carved on Saint Tarcisius's grave; it says that the boy died in 257. "Benedict XVI: General Audience."

224 "Benedict XVI: General Audience."

225 "Benedict XVI: General Audience."

226 "Benedict XVI: General Audience."

227 "Benedict XVI: General Audience."

228 Check, "Viva Cristo Rey!"

229 Olvera, "Evolución Histórica de la Bandera Mexicana."

230 Rubio, "Saint José Luis Sánchez del Río."

231 Check, "Viva Cristo Rey!"

232 Check, "Viva Cristo Rey!"

233 Ferreira, *Blessed José Luis Sánchez del Río*, 16.

234 Rubio, "Saint José Luis Sánchez del Río."

235 Ferreira, *Blessed José Luis Sánchez del Río*, 16.

236 Ferreira, 16.

237 Ferreira, 16.

238 "José Anacleto González Flores and eight Companions."

239 Rubio, "Saint José Luis Sánchez del Río."

240 Rubio, "Saint José Luis Sánchez del Río."

241 Ferreira, *Blessed José Luis Sánchez del Río,* 18.

242 Ferreira, 19.

243 Ferreira, 19.

244 Ferreira, 19.

245 Ferreira, 19.

246 José's father was in Guadalajara, desperately trying to raise money for a ransom to have José released. "José Anacleto González Flores and eight Companions"; Ferreira, *Blessed José Luis Sánchez del Río,* 20.

247 Ferreira, *Blessed José Luis Sánchez del Río,* 20.

[248] Ferreira, 20.

[249] José's body laid there for eighteen years until it was transferred to the Church of the Sacred Heart, where it laid for fifty years. Ferreira, 21.

[250] "Apostolic letter by which the Supreme Pontiff Benedict XVI has raised to the glory of the altars the servants of God."

[251] "Raising a Martyr: Interview with Marianna Popiełuszko."

[252] "Raising a Martyr: Interview with Marianna Popiełuszko."

[253] Sikorska, *A Martyr for Truth*, 24.

[254] "Raising a Martyr: Interview with Marianna Popiełuszko."

[255] Brien, *Blessed Jerzy Popiełuszko*, 24.

[256] "Raising a Martyr: Interview with Marianna Popiełuszko."

[257] Associated Press, "Texts of Molotoff Talks Explaining Military Action."

[259] Tadeusz, *Poland's Holocaust*, 305.

[260] "Estimated pre-war Jewish population and estimated number of murdered Jews per country during the Holocaust from 1930 to 1945."

[261] Craughwell, "The Gentile Holocaust."

[262] Berthon, *Warlords*, 285.

[263] "Raising a Martyr: Interview with Marianna Popiełuszko."

[264] LaMay, *The Life of St. Maximilian Kolbe*, 16.

[265] LaMay, 26.

[266] LaMay, 22–23.

[267] LaMay, 26.

[268] Kengor, *A Pope and a President*, 21.

[269] Gorny, *Fatima's Mysteries*, 80.

[270] Byrnes, "Bolshevik Persecution of the Catholic Church."

[271] "Did Freemasonry Really Begin in 1717?"

[272] Vennari, *The Permanent Instruction of the Alta Vendita*.

[273] Pope Leo XIII, *Dall'alto dell'Apostolico Seggio*.

[274] Pope Leo XIII, *Dall'alto dell'Apostolico Seggio*.

[275] Smith, *Saint Maximilian Kolbe*, 15.

[276] Foster, *Mary's Knight*, 143.

277 Tasca, *The Writings of St. Maximilian Maria Kolbe*, 2317.
278 Tasca, 2251.
279 Tasca, 2317.
280 Tasca, 71.
281 Smith, *Saint Maximilian Kolbe*, 38.
282 Smith, 40–42.
283 Smith, 49–61.
284 Pope Pius XI, *Divini Redemptoris.*
285 Pope Pius XI, *Mit Brennender Sorge.*
286 Smith, *Saint Maximilian Kolbe*, 43.
287 LaMay, 63.
288 "Maximilian Kolbe Biography."
289 LaMay, *The Life of St. Maximilian Kolbe*, 67–74.
290 LaMay, 82.
291 Tasca, *The Writings of St. Maximilian Maria Kolbe*, 2299.
292 LaMay, *The Life of St. Maximilian Kolbe*, 86–87.
293 LaMay, 86–87.
294 LaMay, 86–87.
295 Tasca, *The Writings of St. Maximilian Maria Kolbe*, 2317.
296 LaMay, *The Life of St. Maximilian Kolbe*, 93.
297 LaMay, 95.
298 LaMay, 95.
299 Nelson, "The 'Poison' of Spiritual Indifference."
300 "Homily for the Canonization of St. Maximilian Kolbe."
301 "[Fr. Jerzy] was refused a passport to travel to Rome in October 1982 for the canonization of the Polish saint, Father Maximilian Kolbe—his own personal hero." Sikorska, *A Martyr for Truth*, 63.
302 "Poland History and Background."
303 "Raising a Martyr: Interview with Marianna Popiełuszko."
304 Sikorska, *A Martyr for Truth*, 19.
305 Materski, "Personal losses and victims of repression under two occupations, 1939-1945," 28.
306 Materski, 9.
307 Piotrowski, *Poland's Holocaust*, 300.

308 Materski, "Personal losses and victims of repression under two occupations, 1939-1945," 30.

309 "Cardinal Wyszyński: Dignity of Every Human Being."

310 "Cardinal Wyszyński: Dignity of Every Human Being."

311 "Warsaw Uprising - WW2 Timeline (August 1st - October 2nd, 1944)."

312 Siekierski, "Remembering the Warsaw Uprising."

313 Craughwell, "The Gentile Holocaust."

314 Brand, *Cardinal Wyszyński*, 80, 87, 88.

315 Brand, 82.

316 Brand, 89.

317 Brand, 156–57.

318 de Souza, "Popes, Poland, and Powerful PR."

319 de Souza, "Popes, Poland, and Powerful PR."

320 Weigel, *Witness to Hope*, 301.

321 Homily at a Mass for the Fatherland, August 1983, in Popiełuszko, *Chemin de ma croix*, 50, cited in Brien, *Blessed Jerzy Popiełuszko*, 54.

322 "Raising a Martyr: Interview with Marianna Popiełuszko."

323 Sikorska, *A Martyr for Truth*, 21–22.

324 Hensler, *Messenger of the Truth*.

325 Kengor, *A Pope and a President*, 179.

326 Kengor, 181.

327 Kengor, 181.

328 Kengor, 185.

329 Kengor, 186.

330 Kengor, *The Devil and Karl Marx*.

331 Marx wrote, "Religion is . . . the opium of the people. The abolition of religion as the illusory happiness of the people is the demand for their real happiness. . . . The criticism of religion disillusions man, so that he will think, act, and fashion his reality like a man who has discarded his illusions and regained his senses, so that he will move around himself as his own true Sun." Marx, "A Contribution to the Critique of Hegel's Philosophy of Right."

[332] Letter quoted by Bernard Lecomte in "So-li-darnosc!": Comment le pape polonaise a renverse le cours de l'histoire", in Les Secrets du Vatican (Paris: Tempus, 2011), 239. Cited in Brien, *Blessed Jerzy Popiełuszko*, 40.

[333] Sikorska, *A Martyr for Truth*, 31.

[334] Sikorska, 32.

[335] Sikorska, 33-34.

[336] Brien, *Blessed Jerzy Popiełuszko*, 50–51.

[337] Homily at a Mass for the Fatherland, September 1982, in Popiełuszko, Chem de ma croix, 58, cited in Brien, *Blessed Jerzy Popiełuszko*, 54.

[338] Brien, *Blessed Jerzy Popiełuszko*, 59.

[339] Homily at a Mass for the Fatherland, March 1983, in Popiełuszko, Chem de ma croix, 58, cited in Brien, *Blessed Jerzy Popiełuszko*, 73.

[340] Brien, *Blessed Jerzy Popiełuszko*, 72.

[341] Brien, 72.

[342] Sikorska, *A Martyr for Truth*, 84–88.

[343] Homily at a Mass for the Fatherland, October 1982, in Popiełuszko, Chem de ma croix, 58, cited in Brien, *Blessed Jerzy Popiełuszko*, 76.

[344] "Over 100,000 attend beatification of Polish priest and martyr."

[345] "Raising a Martyr: Interview with Marianna Popiełuszko."

[346] Spink, *Mother Teresa*, 3–4.

[347] *CCC* 1216, citing St. Gregory of Nazianzus, Oratio 40, 3-4: J.P Migne, ed., Patrologia Graeca (Paris, 1857-1866) 36, 361C.

[348] Spink, *Mother Teresa*, 7–8.

[349] Spink, 6.

[350] Spink, 4. Lazar was three years older than Agnes.

[351] Spink, 5.

[352] Vardey, *Mother Teresa*, xx.

[353] Spink, *Mother Teresa*, 6–10.

[354] Spink, 9–10.

355 From a letter Zelie wrote to her daughter, Pauline, in May of 1877. O'Hearn, *Parents of the Saints*, 86.

356 Thérèse was named after her sister, Marie-Melanie-Thérèse, who died at seven weeks old. O'Hearn, *Parents of the Saints*, 187.

357 St. Thérèse of Lisieux, *Story of a Soul*, 6.

358 St. Thérèse of Lisieux, 7.

359 St. Thérèse of Lisieux, 10–11.

360 St. Thérèse of Lisieux, 10.

361 O'Hearn, *Parents of the Saints*, 143.

362 "Sister Marie of the Sacred Heart Marie Louise Martin."

363 St. Thérèse of Lisieux, *Story of a Soul*, 32.

364 St. Thérèse of Lisieux, 36.

365 St. Thérèse of Lisieux, 36.

366 St. Thérèse of Lisieux, 37.

367 St. Thérèse of Lisieux, 45.

368 St. Thérèse of Lisieux, 54.

369 St. Thérèse of Lisieux, 55.

370 St. Thérèse of Lisieux, 112–13.

371 St. Thérèse of Lisieux, 182.

372 St. Thérèse of Lisieux, 170.

373 "To be Thy Spouse, O my Jesus, to be a daughter of Carmel, and by my union with Thee to be the mother of souls, should not all this content me? And yet other vocations make themselves felt—I feel called to the Priesthood and to the Apostolate—I would be a Martyr, a Doctor of the Church. I should like to accomplish the most heroic deeds—the spirit of the Crusader burns within me, and I long to die on the field of battle in defense of Holy Church." St. Thérèse of Lisieux, 154.

374 "I look only at the present, I forget the past, and I take good care not to forestall the future. When we yield to discouragement or despair it is usually because we think too much about the past and future." St. Thérèse of Lisieux, 174.

375 St. Thérèse of Lisieux, 12.

376 St. Thérèse of Lisieux, 122.

377 St. Thérèse of Lisieux, 223.
378 St. Thérèse of Lisieux, 131.
379 St. Thérèse of Lisieux, 173.
380 St. Thérèse of Lisieux, 183–84.
381 St. Thérèse of Lisieux, 189.
382 "St. Thérèse of Lisieux: Doctor of the Universal Church."
383 Spink, *Mother Teresa*, 14.
384 Spink, 14–15.
385 Spink, 16–17.
386 Spink, 18.
387 Spink, 18.
388 Spink, 328.
389 Spink, 300.
390 Spink, 22.
391 Spink, 23.
392 Spink, 25.
393 Spink, 28.
394 Spink, 36.
395 Spink, 324.
396 Spink, 55.
397 Spink, 24.
398 Spink, 42.
399 Spink, 42–50.
400 Spink, 143.
401 Spink, Appendix A.
402 Spink, 24
403 Spink, 85.
404 Spink, 324.
405 She had received some public recognition, especially in India. In 1962, she was one of twenty-five recipients of India's Padma Shri Award. "List of Padma Shri Award Recipients (1954-2022)."
406 Spink, *Mother Teresa*, 165.
407 "P. Paul VI Presentation of the Pope John XXIII Peace Prize (Vatican) to Mother Teresa, dated January 6th, 1971."

[408] Spink, *Mother Teresa*, 161.

[409] "Something Beautiful for God."

[410] Conlin, "Something Beautiful for God by Malcolm Muggeridge."

[411] Spink, *Mother Teresa*, 165–66.

[412] "Mother Teresa: Catholic Nun and Missionary."

[413] "Albert Schweitzer International Prizes Ceremony at UNC-Wilmington."

[414] "Major Awards Received by Mother Teresa."

[415] "The Nobel Peace Prize 1979."

[416] "Mother Teresa Acceptance Speech."

[417] *CCC* 2271, 2272.

[418] *CCC* 2270.

[419] *CCC* 2273.

[420] "54 years of the Pill (on the NHS), and how Birmingham women got it first."

[421] "Conceptions in England and Wales: 2013."

[422] *CCC* 776.

[423] Pope Paul VI, *Humanae Vitae* (July 25, 1968).

[424] "Declaration on Procured Abortion."

[425] Pope John Paul II, *Evangelium Vitae* (March 25, 1995).

[426] "Rome Synod to End by Reaffirming Ban on Birth Control and Abortion; 'Prophetic Dimensions' Cardinal Cooke Criticizes U.S."

[427] Spink, *Mother Teresa*, 177.

[428] Spink, 186.

[429] Spink, 190.

[430] Spink, 266.

[431] Spink, 276.

[432] Spink, 253.

[433] Kengor, "How Mother Teresa Challenged Hillary Clinton on Abortion."

[434] Noonan, "Still, Small Voice."

[435] Noonan, "Still, Small Voice."

436   Noonan, "Still, Small Voice."

437   Kengor, "How Mother Teresa Challenged Hillary Clinton on Abortion."

438   Kengor, "How Mother Teresa Challenged Hillary Clinton on Abortion."

439   "Beatification of Mother Teresa of Calcutta, Homily of His Holiness John Paul II."

440   "Holy Mass and Canonization of Blessed Mother Teresa of Calcutta."

441   St. Thérèse of Lisieux, *Story of a Soul*, 131.

442   *CCC* 1996, 1998.

443   *CCC* 1023.

444   Lewis, *The Screwtape Letters*, 174.

Other Resources for Catholic Parents

Parenting

Parenting for Eternity: A Guide to Raising Children in Holy Mother Church by Conor Gallagher (TAN Books, 2021)

Raising Catholic Kids for Their Vocations by John Grabowski, PhD (TAN Books, 2019)

Ten Ways to Destroy the Imagination of Your Child by Anthony Esolen, PhD (ISI Books, 2013)

Defending Boyhood: How Building Forts, Reading Stories, Playing Ball, and Praying to God Can Change the World by Anthony Esolen, PhD (TAN Books, 2019)

Strong Mothers, Strong Sons: Lessons Mothers Need to Raise Extraordinary Men by Meg Meeker, MD (Ignatius Press, 2015)

Raising a Strong Daughter in a Toxic Culture: 11 Steps to Keep Her Happy, Healthy, and Safe by Meg Meeker, MD (Ignatius Press, 2021)

*Made This Way: How to Prepare Kids to Face Today's Tough
Moral Issues* by Leila Miller and Trent Horn (Catholic
Answers, 2018)

*Glow Kids: How Screen Addiction Is Hijacking Our Kids
- and How to Break the Trance* by Nicholas Kardaras
(Macmillan Publishers, 2016)

Way to Happiness by Archbishop Fulton J. Sheen, DD
(TAN Books, 2022, a compilation of essays written
during Archbishop Sheen's life, 1895-1975)

Under Siege: No Finer Time to be a Faithful Catholic by
Austin Ruse (Sophia Institute Press, 2021)

*Parents of the Saints: The Hidden Heroes Behind Our Favorite
Saints* by Patrick O'Hearn (TAN Books, 2020)

Catholic Education

*Renewing Catholic Schools: How to Regain a Catholic Vision
for a Secular Age* by Andrew Seeley, R. Jared Staudt,
Elisabeth Sullivan, Michael Van Hecke, and Rosemary
Vander Weele (Catholic Education Press, 2020)

The Holy See's Teaching on Catholic Schools by Archbishop J.
Michael Miller (Sophia Institute Press, 2006)

Charter of the Rights of the Family (The Holy See, 1983)

Catholic School Playbook (catholicschoolplaybook.com)

Institute for Catholic Liberal Education
(catholicliberaleducation.org)

TAN Academy (tanacademy.com)

Curricular Materials

The Story of Civilization by Phillip Campbell (history textbooks by TAN Books)

Spirit of Truth (religion curriculum by Sophia Institute Press)

History and science textbooks by Catholic Textbook Project

For Kids

Treasure Box books by the Maryknoll Sisters (TAN Books, 1957)

Books on the lives of saints by Mary Fabyan Windeatt (TAN Books, 1940s and 1950s)

Books on the lives of saints by Louis de Wohl (Ignatius Press, 1940s to 1960s)

Glory Stories by Holy Heroes (holyheroes.com)

Shining Light Dolls (shininglightdolls.com)

Dolls from Heaven (dollsfromheaven.com)

Bibliography

"54 years of the Pill (on the NHS), and how Birmingham women got it first." *The Guardian*, accessed March 11, 2022, https://www.theguardian.com/science/the-h-word /2015/dec/04/54-years-of-the-pill-on-the-nhs-and-how -birmingham-women-got-it-first.

"Albert Schweitzer International Prizes Ceremony at UNC-Wilmington." Internet Archive, accessed February 27, 2022, https://archive.org/details/uncw_schweit zerawards1975_a.

"Alexandria." Catholic Answers, accessed July 28, 2022, https://www.catholic.com/encyclopedia/Alexandria.

"Apostolic letter by which the Supreme Pontiff Benedict XVI has raised to the glory of the altars the servants of God." Daily Bulletin of the Holy See Press Office, November 15, 2005, https://www.vatican.va/content/benedict-xvi/en/apost _letters/documents/hf_ben-xvi_apl_20051115_beatif ication-messico.html.

Associated Press. "Texts of Molotoff Talks Explaining Military Action." *New York Times*, September 18, 1939,

https://www.nytimes.com/1939/09/18/archives/texts-of
-molotoff-talks-explaining-military-action.html.

"Beatification of Mother Teresa of Calcutta, Homily of His
Holiness John Paul II." The Holy See, October 19, 2003,
https://www.vatican.va/content/john-paul-ii/en/homi
lies/2003/documents/hf_jp-ii_hom_20031019_mother
-theresa.html.

Benedictine Convent of Clyde Missouri. *St. Michael the
Archangel.* Charlotte: TAN Books, 2012.

"Benedict XVI: General Audience." Daily Bulletin of the
Holy See Press Office, August 4, 2010, https://www
.vatican.va/content/benedict-xvi/en/audiences/2010
/documents/hf_ben-xvi_aud_20100804.html.

Berthon, Simon and Joanna Potts. *Warlords: An Extraor-
dinary Re-creation of World War II Through the Eyes and
Minds of Hitler, Churchill, Roosevelt, and Stalin.* Da Capo
Press, 2007.

"Blessed Anacleto González Flores." CatholicSaints.Info,
accessed November 24, 2021, https://catholicsaints.info/
blessed-anacleto-González-flores/.

"Bl. Analceto González Flores: Spiritual Leader of the Cristeros."
The Remnant Newspaper, October 17, 2018, accessed
December 13, 2021, https://remnantnewspaper.com/web
/index.php/articles/item/4144-bl-anacleto-González-flo
res-spiritual-leader-of-the-cristeros?tmpl=component.

Brand, William R. and Katarzyna Mroczkowska-Brand.
Cardinal Wyszyński: A Biography. Translated by Andrej
Micewski. San Diego: Harcourt Brace Jovanovich, 1984.

Breslin, Carole. "Catholic Heroes… Blessed Anacelto Gonzales Flores." The Wanderer, accessed November 26, 2021,

https://thewandererpress.com/saints/catholic-heroes
-blessed-anacleto-González-flores/.

Brien, Bernard and Charles Wright. *Blessed Jerzy Popiełuszko: Truth Versus Totalitarianism*. Translated by Michael J. Miller. San Francisco: Ignatius Press, 2018.

Byrnes, Donia. "Bolshevik Persecution of the Catholic Church." The Student Historical Journal 1987-1988, accessed October 7, 2021, http://people.loyno.edu/~history /journal/1987-8/byrnes.htm.

"Cardinal Wyszyński: Dignity of Every Human Being." Exaudi Catholic News, accessed October 10, 2021, https:// www.exaudi.org/cardinal-Wyszyński-dignity-of-every -human-being/.

Carlson, Amelia Monroe. "Abortion: Child sacrifice to the god of ourselves." Catholic365, accessed November 6, 2021, https://www.catholic365.com/article/11390/abortion -child-sacrifice-to-the-god-of-ourselves.html.

Carroll, Warren H. *The Cleaving of Christendom*. Vol. 4 of *A History of Christendom*. Front Royal: Christendom Press, 2000.

———. *The Founding of Christendom*. Vol. 1 of *A History of Christendom*. Front Royal: Christendom Publications, 1985.

———. *The Glory of Christendom*. Vol. 3 of *A History of Christendom*. Front Royal: Christendom Publications, 1993.

Catechism of the Catholic Church: Second Edition. Double-day, 1995.

"Catholic Church and the Age of Discovery." The Spiritual Life, accessed November 7, 2021, https://slife.org/catholic-church-and-the-age-of-discovery/.

Cerrone, Michael. *For God and Country: The Heroic Life and Martyrdom of St. Joan of Arc.* Manchester: Sophia Institute Press, 2015.

Chavez, Eduardo. *Our Lady of Guadalupe and Saint Juan Diego: The Historical Evidence.* Translated by Carmen Trevino and Veronica Montano. Rowman & Littlefield Publishers, Inc., 2006.

Check, Christopher. "Viva Cristo Rey! The Cristeros Versus the Mexican Revolution." Catholic Culture, accessed December 18, 2021, https://www.catholicculture.org/culture/library/view.cfm?id=7826.

Chesterton, G. K. *The Catholic Church and Conversion.* New York: MacMillan Company, 1926.

"Claims about the Tilma and the Image." Truths of the Image, accessed December 12, 2021, http://www.truthsoftheimage.org/tr/en/claims/9bomb.html.

Conlin, Richard. "Something Beautiful for God by Malcolm Muggeridge." The Prodigal Catholic, July 8, 2015, https://prodigalcatholic.com/2015/07/08/something-beautiful-for-god-by-malcolm-muggeridge/.

"Conceptions in England and Wales: 2013." Office for National Statistics, accessed March 11, 2022, https://www.ons.gov.uk/peoplepopulationandcommunity/birthsdeathsandmarriages/conceptionandfertilityrates/bulletins/conceptionstatistics/2015-02-24.

"Constantine the Great." Catholic Answers, accessed September 24, 2022, https://www.catholic.com/encyclopedia/constantine-the-great.

Craughwell, Thomas J. "The Gentile Holocaust." Catholic Culture, accessed October 7, 2021, https://www.catholicculture.org/culture/library/view.cfm?recnum=472.

de Souza, Raymond J. "Popes, Poland, and Powerful PR." *National Catholic Register*, accessed October 10, 2021, https://www.ncregister.com/news/popes-poland-and-powerful-pr.

Delaney, John I. *Dictionary of Saints*. New York: Doubleday, 1980.

"Declaration on Procured Abortion." Sacred Congregation for the Doctrine of the Faith, The Holy See, accessed March 6, 2022, https://www.vatican.va/roman_curia/congregations/cfaith/documents/rc_con_cfaith_doc_19741118_declaration-abortion_en.html.

"Did Freemasonry Really Begin in 1717?" Freemasonry Community (website), accessed September 23, 2022, https://freemasonscommunity.life/did-freemasonry-really-begin-in-1717.

"Diocletian." Catholic Answers, accessed July 28, 2022, https://www.catholic.com/encyclopedia/Diocletian.

Dominic, Br. "Saint Miguel Pro, A Modern Martyr." Catholicism.org, October 7, 2004, https://catholicism.org/padre-pro.html.

Elarde, Paul. "Our Lady of Guadalupe, Our Queen, Our Mother: the Graces of the Blessed Virgin Mary." Cradio (app), April 26, 2013.

"Estimated pre-war Jewish population and estimated number of murdered Jews per country during the Holocaust from 1930 to 1945." Statista, accessed October 7, 2021, https://www.statista.com/statistics/1070564/jewish-populations-deaths-by-country/.

Ferreira, Cornelia R. *Blessed José Luis Sánchez del Río: Cristero Boy Martyr.* Toronto: Canisius Books, 2006.

Foster, Claude R. *Mary's Knight: The Mission and Martyrdon of Saint Maksymilian Maria Kolbe.* United States of America: West Chester Univerity Press, 2002.

Gorny, Grzegorz and Janusz Rosikon. *Fatima's Mysteries: Mary's Message to the Modern Age.* San Francisco: Ignatius Press, 2016 .

Hensler, Paul and Paul G. Hensler (Producers), Tony Haines (Director), Martin Sheen (Narrator). *Messenger of the Truth.* FilmRise Movies, 2013. See: https://www.youtube.com/watch?v=0VrMDIHvi5o.

"Her Battle Standard." Joan of Arc (website), accessed September 25, 2022, https://www.saint-joan-of-arc.com/banner.htm.

Hoffman, Matthew Cullinan. "The true story of For Greater Glory." The Catholic World Report, July 6, 2012, https://www.catholicworldreport.com/2012/07/06/the-true-story-of/.

"Holy Mass and Canonization of Blessed Mother Teresa of Calcutta." The Holy See, September 4, 2016, https://www.vatican.va/content/francesco/en/homilies/2016/documents/papa-francesco_20160904_omelia-canonizzazione-madre-teresa.html.

"Homily for the Canonization of St. Maximilian Kolbe."
Society of the Holy Rosary, accessed October 7, 2021,
https://www.societyoftheholyrosary.com/homily
-for-the-canonization-of-st-maximilian-kolbe/.

Jasper, William F. "Movie on Cristeros War Exposes Mexican
Govt.'s Anti-Christian Campaign." The New American,
June 8, 2012, https://thenewamerican.com/movie-on-crist
eros-war-exposes-mexican-govts-anti-christian-cam
paign/.

"Jean Duke of Alençon." Maid of Heaven (website), accessed
July 12, 2022, http://www.maidofheaven.com/joanofarc
_alencon.asp.

"Joan's Leap for Freedom." Maid of Heaven (website), accessed
August 8, 2022, www.maidofheaven.com/joanofarc
_escape_attempt_bdk.asp.

John Paul II. "Address by the Holy Father John Paul II," July
25, 2002.

"José Anacleto González Flores and eight Companions."
The Holy See (website), accessed October 29, 2021,
https://www.vatican.va/news_services/liturgy/saints/ns
_lit_doc_20051120_anacleto-González_en.html.

Kengor, Paul. *A Pope and a President: John Paul II, Ronald
Reagan, and the Extraordinary Untold Story of the 20th Century.* Wilmington: ISI Books, 2017.

———. "How Mother Teresa Challenged Hillary Clinton on
Abortion." *National Catholic Register*, September 2, 2016,
https://www.ncregister.com/news/how-mother-teresa
-challenged-hillary-clinton-on-abortion.

———. *The Devil and Karl Marx: Communism's Long March of Death, Deception, and Infiltration.* Gastonia, NC: TAN Books, 2020.

Kerkhove, Ray. "Dark Religion? Aztec Perspectives on Human Sacrifice." Core, accessed November 6, 2021, https://core.ac.uk/download/pdf/229403978.pdf.

Kosloski, Philip. "The 18-year-old who defied an emperor." Aleteia, November 25, 2017, https://aleteia.org/2017/11/25/the-18-year-old-girl-who-defied-an-emperor/.

LaMay, William. *The Life of St. Maximilian Kolbe: Apostle of Mass Communications.* William LaMay, 2019.

Lewis, C. S. *The Screwtape Letters: Annotated Edition.* HarperCollins, 2013 .

"List of Padma Shri Award Recipients (1954-2022)." GKGIGS, accessed February 27, 2022, https://www.gkgigs.com/padma-shri-award-recipients/.

"Major Awards Received by Mother Teresa." Mother Teresa (website), accessed February 27, 2022, https://mthrteresa.tripod.com/awards.html.

Marison, Fiscar. *A Popular Abridgement of The Mystical City of God by Venerable Mary of Agreda.* Charlotte: TAN Books, 1978.

Marx, Karl. "A Contribution to the Critique of Hegel's Philosophy of Right." Paris: Deutsch-Französische Jahrbücher, February 7 and 10, 1844.

Materski, Wojciech and Tomasz Szarota. "Personal losses and victims of repression under two occupations, 1939-1945. Institute of National Remembrance." Warsaw: 2009.

"Maximilian Kolbe Biography." Biography Online, accessed November 7, 2021, https://www.biographyonline.net/spiritual/maximilian-kolbe.html.

Medina, Luis. "When the Marxists Tried to Take Over Mexico." OnePeterFive, August 31, 2021, https://onepeterfive.com/when-the-marxists-tried-takeover-mexico/.

Encyclopedia.com, s.v. "Mora Y Del Rio, José (1854-1928)," accessed November 26, 2021.

"Mother Teresa Acceptance Speech." The Nobel Prize, accessed March 2, 2022, https://www.nobelprize.org/prizes/peace/1979/teresa/acceptance-speech/.

"Mother Teresa: Catholic Nun and Missionary." Templeton Prize, accessed February 27, 2022, https://www.harpercollins.com/products/something-beautiful-for-god-malcolm-muggeridge?variant=32117235384354.

Murphy, James T. *Saints and Sinners in the Cristero War: Stories of Martyrdom from Mexico*. San Francisco: Ignatius Press, 2019.

Nelson, Matt. "The 'Poison' of Spiritual Indifference." Catholic Answers, accessed October 7, 2021, https://www.wordonfire.org/resources/blog/the-poison-of-religious-indifference/30149/.

Noonan, Peggy. "Still, Small Voice." *Crisis Magazine*, February 1, 1998, https://peggynoonan.com/71/.

O'Hearn, Patrick. *Parents of the Saints: The Hidden Heroes Behind Our Favorite Saints*. Gastonia, NC: TAN Books, 2020.

Olvera, Alfonso. "Evolución Histórica de la Bandera Mexicana." Inside Mexico, October 1, 2018, https://

www.inside-mexico.com/evolucion-historica-de-la
-bandera-mexicana/2/.

"Over 100,000 attend beatification of Polish priest and martyr." Catholic News Agency, June 7, 2010, https://www.catholicnewsagency.com/news/19919/over-100000 -attend-beatification-of-polish-priest-and-martyr.

"P. Paul VI Presentation of the Pope John XXIII Peace Prize (Vatican) to Mother Teresa, dated January 6th, 1971." Mother Teresa (website), accessed February 27, 2022, https://www.motherteresa.org/paulvi.html.

Pernoud, Regine. *Joan of Arc: By Herself and Her Witnesses.* United States: Scarborough House, 1982.

Peterson, Larry. "Famous last words: A martyr of the bloody Cristero War forgives his persecutors." Aleteia, January 15, 2017, https://aleteia.org/2017/01/15/famous-last -words-a-martyr-of-the-bloody-cristero-war-forgives-his -persecutors/#.

Piotrowski, Tadeusz. *Poland's Holocaust: Ethnic Strife, Collaboration with Occupying Forces and Genocide in the Second Republic, 1918-1947.* McFarland & Company: 1997.

"Poland History and Background." Education Encyclopedia State University, https://education.stateuniversity.com /pages/1209/Poland-HISTORY-BACKGROUND.html.

Pope Leo XIII, *Dall'alto dell'Apostolico Seggio* [Encyclical on Freemasonry in Italy]. October 15, 1890, accessed October 10, 2021, https://www.vatican.va/content/leo -xiii/en/encyclicals/documents/hf_l-xiii_enc_18901015 _apostolico-seggio.html.

Pope Pius XI, *Divini Redemptoris* [Encyclical on Atheistic Communism]. March 19, 1937, https://www.vatican

.va/content/pius-xi/en/encyclicals/documents/hf_p-xi
_enc_19370319_divini-redemptoris.html.

Pope Pius XI, *Iniquis Afflictisque*, November 18, 1926, https://
www.vatican.va/content/pius-xi/en/encyclicals/doc
uments/hf_p-xi_enc_18111926_iniquis-afflictisque.
html.

Pope Pius XI, *Mit Brennender Sorge*. [Encyclical on the
Church and the German Reich], March 14, 1937.

"Quis Ut Deus, Who's Like God." StMichael (website),
accessed June 19, 2022, https://stmichael.com/.

"Raising a Martyr: Interview with Marianna Popiełuszko."
EWTN, accessed October 7, 2021, https://www.ewtn
.com/catholicism/library/raising-a-martyr-5981.

"Relación Política México – Rusia." Relaciones Exteriores:
Secretaria de Relaciones Exteriores, accessed December
11, 2021, https://embamex.sre.gob.mx/rusia/index.php
/es/relacion-bilateral.

"Rome Synod to End by Reaffirming Ban on Birth Control
and Abortion; 'Prophetic Dimensions' Cardinal Cooke
Criticizes U.S." *The New York Times*, October 24, 1980,
https://www.nytimes.com/1980/10/24/archives/rome
-synod-to-end-by-reaffirming-ban-on-birth-control-and
-abortion.html.

Rubio, Elias. "Saint José Luis Sánchez del Río: Hero for Christ
the King." The American Society for the Defense of Tradition, Family, and Property, October 16, 2016, https://www
.tfp.org/saint-José-luis-sanchez-del-rio-hero-christ-king/.

"Saint Catherine of Alexandria." Catholic Online, accessed
July 28, 2022, https://www.catholic.org/saints/saint.php?
saint_id=341.

"Siege of Orléans." Weapons and Warfare (website), accessed July 10, 2022, https://weaponsandwarfare.com/2021/06/28/the-siege-of-Orléans/.

Siekierski, Maciej. "Remembering the Warsaw Uprising." Hoover Institution, accessed October 20, 2021, https://www.hoover.org/research/remembering-warsaw-uprising.

Sikorska, Grazyna. *A Martyr for Truth: Jerzy Popiełuszko.* London: Fount Paperbacks, 1985.

"Sister Marie of the Sacred Heart Marie Louise Martin." Martin Sisters (website), accessed January 30, 2022, https://martinsisters.org/sister_marie_of_the_sacred_heart.html.

Smith, Jeremiah J. *Saint Maximilian Kolbe: Knight of the Immaculata.* Charlotte, TAN Books, 1998.

"Something Beautiful for God." HarperCollins Publishers, accessed February 27, 2022, https://www.harpercollins.com/products/something-beautiful-for-god-malcolm-muggeridge?variant=32117235384354.

Spink, Kathryn. *Mother Teresa: An Authorized Biography.* New York: HarperCollins, 2011.

Spoto, Donald. *Joan: The Mysterious Life of the Heretic who Became a Saint.* New York: HarperOne, 2007.

Stearns, Peter N. "Happy Children: A Modern Emotional Commitment." Frontiers, accessed November 25, 2022, https://www.frontiersin.org/articles/10.3389/fpsyg.2019.02025/full.

"St. Juan Diego." Catholic Online, accessed November 27, 2021, https://www.catholic.org/saints/saint.php?saint_id=73.

"St. Thérèse of Lisieux: Doctor of the Universal Church." St. Thérèse of Lisieux: A Gateway (website), accessed

February 6, 2022, http://www.Thérèseoflisieux.org/
doctor-of-the-universal-church/.

Tadeusz, Piotrowski. *Poland's Holocaust: Ethnic Strife, Collaboration with Occupying Forces and Genocide.* McFarland, 1997 .

Tasca, Marc. *The Writings of St. Maximilian Maria Kolbe: Volume II.* Rome: Associazone Pubblica Internazionale Milizia dell'Immacolata, 2016 .

"The Battle of the Herrings." Jeanne d'arc la pucelle (website), citing historian Regine Pernoud, accessed July 3, 2022, https://www.jeanne-darc.info/location/herrings/.

"The Cristero War." Explorando Mexico, accessed December 12, 2021, http://www.explorandomexico.com /about-mexico/4/154/.

"The Nobel Peace Prize 1979." The Nobel Prize, accessed February 27, 2022, https://www.nobelprize.org/prizes /peace/1979/summary/.

Thérèse of Lisieux, St. *Story of a Soul.* Huntington, Indiana: Our Sunday Visitor, 2018.

Vardey, Lucinda. *Mother Teresa: A Simple Path.* New York: Ballantine Books, 1995.

Vennari, John. *The Permanent Instruction of the Alta Vendita.* Rockford, IL: TAN Books, 1999.

Villa, Carmen Elena. "St. José Sánchez del Río: The boy who died of love for Christ the King." Denver Catholic, October 25, 2016, https://denvercatholic.org/st-José-de -jesus-sanchez-del-rio-boy-died-love-christ-king/.

"Warsaw Uprising - WW2 Timeline (August 1st - October 2nd, 1944)." Second World War History, accessed

October 10, 2012, https://www.secondworldwarhistory .com/warsaw-uprising.php.

Weigel, George. *Witness to Hope: The Biography of Pope John Paul II*. New York: HarperCollins, 1999.

Index